Daniel Henderson's book *Fresh Encounters* could revolutionize the way every pastor does ministry. Church leaders will see prayer in a whole new light and with renewed motivation. I do not know of a more practical resource to spark a spirit of genuine revival in a congregation.

—Dr. Jerry Falwell
Pastor, Thomas Road Baptist Church

It is an extraordinary thing to find a local pastor so distinguished by a life of prayer and leading his church to be a benchmark in the real work of prayer. Dr. Daniel Henderson is such a person. It is our privilege to look inside his life and ministry through this book and read about not only how to have a life of prayer, but how to lead your church into a being a church of prayer . . . a church built on prayer. I enthusiastically commend this book to you. At the same time I thank Dr. Henderson for making the extra effort of writing it. I believe this book has the potential of powerfully changing a multitude of churches God's way.

—Dr. Bob Ricker
President, Baptist General Conference (1987–2003)

Daniel Henderson knows how to lead a church in prayer. As a successful pastor, he has learned the necessity of modeling a strong prayer life, training effective prayer leaders, and conducting powerful church prayer meetings. You can learn to do the same. This book will show you how. *Fresh Encounters* will inspire, equip, and envision you to the New Testament realities of a church on her knees. Don't stand on the sidelines any longer, just because you don't know what to do. Open the pages of this book and discover how you can lead your church into a fresh encounter with the living God.

—Cheryl Sacks
Co-founder of BridgeBuilders Intl. Leadership Network
Author of *The Prayer-Saturated Church*

Daniel is the man to write on prayer. It's the passion of his life. We been blessed to spend many hours on my knees with him have also seen him leading a whole church in effective of human methods, this book is desperate the promises that God has attached t for those who desire to walk the path

...cArthur
Pastor/Tea ...munity Church
...You Radio Broadcast

Daniel Henderson does not study prayer; he breathes it. This book not only called me to prayer, it drove me to my knees. The hunger for the presence of God is palpable in this book, and Dr. Henderson's thirst for righteousness is contagious. Do not read this book casually. It will call you to new levels of intimacy with God.

—Dr. Ergun Mehmet Caner
Professor of Theology and Church History, Liberty University
Author of the Gold Medallion-winning book *Unveiling Islam*

Daniel Henderson knows what he is talking about when he shares about prayer. I have watched in amazement as God has used him to awaken the sleeping church to the kind of real, vital, fresh prayer that we first read about in the book of Acts. I commend this book as a *must read* for anyone searching for the awakening of their church through a Holy Spirit driven prayer movement.

—Hans Finzel,
President of World Venture
Author of *The Top Ten Mistakes Leaders Make*

As one who has spent over two decades praying for a massive Christ-awakening in the church, and traveling the world gathering others to do the same, I could not be more delighted with any book on prayer than I am with *Fresh Encounters*. Not only does it refresh our vision for what a true awakening looks like, but it provides invaluable insights and tools for those who are so key to every fresh encounter with Christ among His people: *spiritual leaders*. Fortunately, as much as any leader I know today, in his own ministry Daniel Henderson has incorporated in extraordinary ways the spiritual and practical dimensions of the renewal of which he writes. The scent of authenticity springs from every page of this book!

—David Bryant
Founder, PROCLAIM HOPE!
Author, *Christ Is All! A Joyful Manifesto on the Supremacy of God's Son*

I confess that I wish that this helpful book had been written a number of years ago. I believe I could have profited greatly from it as I attempted to help the congregations I served to become more effective in prayer. At the same time, I am delighted it has been written now. I recommend it to you highly.

—Paul Cedar
Chairman, Mission America

Simple and straightforward, practical and personal, written by a man who has done and is doing it. This is the best source I know of to help a congregation really become a house of prayer. The chapters on "hindrances" alone are worth the price of the book. A great "proof of this pudding" for me has been when I have been with people who have been under Daniel's prayer leadership. I have consistently heard them comment about how much more they loved Jesus because of their times of prayer. They did not point to the vehicles of prayer, they pointed to the destination.

— Dennis Fuqua
Executive Director, International Renewal Ministries

Many pastors are saying, "I want my church to be a house of prayer, but I don't know how to make it happen. I don't know how to move from here to there." This is the tool you have been waiting for. Written by a pastor who has walked it out, this book is the map he has drawn for those on the same journey.

— Jennifer Kennedy Dean
Executive Director, The Praying Life Foundation
Author of *Live a Praying Life*

I share Daniel Henderson's passion to see "pastor-led, local church-focused movements of worship-based prayer." Daniel re-introduced me to the importance of corporate prayer and taught me to pray in 4/4 time. This book is a must read for church leaders who are serious about truly getting their church in touch with the living God.

— Rev. Terry Cuthbert
President, Fellowship of Evangelical Baptist Churches in Canada

On two occasions I have had the opportunity to speak in Daniel Henderson's church. Both times I have sensed the presence of God as soon as I stepped foot on their campus. I sensed it too in his people— they are loaded with joy! The reason: his church prays—*together*. Pastor or prayer leader, nothing will change your church more than developing a vibrant, passion-filled corporate prayer meeting. This book will give you the encouragement, challenge, and principles to take you there.

— Jonathan Graf
President, Church Prayer Leaders Network
Editor of *My House Shall Be a House of Prayer*

Perhaps the most strategic issue facing church leadership today is how to initiate and sustain a genuine work of God in a specific geographic community. Daniel Henderson, with great clarity and precision, lays out the essence of such an awakening in *Fresh Encounters*. Don't miss this one.

—Joseph C. Aldrich
President Emeritus, Multnomah Bible College and Biblical Seminary
Founder, International Renewal Ministries/PrayerSummits.Net

Daniel Henderson has sounded the trumpet call to prayer summits in the local church. Rekindling of faith and renewed passion for Christ become the experience of individuals, families, and an entire congregation as you read this story about one church engaged in prayer summits for more than a decade.

—Luis Bush
International Director, World Inquiry

Here is a book that can truly change lives! As a cancer survivor, I know well the power of prayer. I have seen the incredible things God can do around the world when His people get on their knees. This book captures the power of true biblical prayer. Prayer that will change you . . . prayer that will change your church . . . prayer that will change the nations!

—Vernon Brewer
President, World Help

Fresh Encounters

EXPERIENCING TRANSFORMATION THROUGH
UNITED WORSHIP-BASED PRAYER

By Daniel Henderson
with Margaret Saylar

NAVPRESS

Discipleship Inside Out™

Discipleship Inside Out

NavPress is the publishing ministry of The Navigators, an international Christian organization and leader in personal spiritual development. NavPress is committed to helping people grow spiritually and enjoy lives of meaning and hope through personal and group resources that are biblically rooted, culturally relevant, and highly practical.

**For a free catalog go to www.NavPress.com
or call 1.800.366.7788 in the United States or 1.800.839.4769 in Canada.**

Dedication

This book is lovingly dedicated to
the praying people of

Arcade Church
Sacramento, California

and

Grace Church
Eden Prairie, Minnesota

Your partnership in the ministry of prayer has delighted
my soul and ignited my vision for His glory.

Acknowledgments

My special thanks to Margaret Saylar for your careful concern in editing and patient support of this project to the very end. I know we both miss your dear husband Dan so very much. He would have been so proud of you.

My deepest love and appreciation to Rosemary, my treasured partner in life and ministry. Without you by my side I would have never been free to soar into so many "fresh encounters" with Jesus.

To Justin, Jordan and Heather—Thanks for encouraging your dad in so many ways, especially by your growing love for the presence of Christ.

It has been my joy to partner with Jon Graf and the wonderful people at *Pray!* Thank you for believing in this project.

Contents

FOREWORD

America is being enveloped by a growing spiritual darkness that seems to be affecting virtually every area of our culture—even much of the church in the Western world. Like a slow-moving blanket of dark smog, this cloud of darkness seems to be gaining momentum day by day.

There is little doubt that there is a desperate need for spiritual renewal in this nation and beyond. However, as Pastor Daniel Henderson asserts, the church often seems to be asleep—especially in regard to the powerful ministry of prayer. Much of the church has become a sleeping giant that needs to become awakened to its potential and spiritual power.

Without a doubt, the church of Jesus Christ is key to combating and overcoming the spiritual darkness that seeks to dominate. Authentic transformation of cities and communities and other societal entities must begin in the lives of the Christians of a nation.

Daniel Henderson understands that prayer is the first major step toward penetrating and then overcoming spiritual darkness. Prayer is not the only thing we do, but it is the first thing we do. It is foundational for bringing light to the darkness.

History would teach us that there will be no revival or spiritual awakening unless churches begin to pray. In addition, most churches will not become houses of prayer unless pastors lead the way through their personal example and through skilled and strategic leadership in prayer.

Daniel Henderson is that kind of a pastor. I have had the privilege of observing Daniel in that important role for a number of years. For more than twenty years he has led congregations to become involved in effective corporate prayer meetings. In fact, the churches that he has served have become models in prayer ministry.

Fresh Encounters is a reflection of Daniel's consistent commitment to raise up competent and confident prayer leaders and people of prayer in the local church. This is not a volume that is based upon theory. To the contrary, it conveys the conviction and implementation of prayer principles by a pastor who has been committed to the important ministry of helping the local church become a house of prayer—in word and deed.

The principles that Daniel presents are practical and proven. The stories are real, deeply inspiring, and motivating. This book will help every pastor and local church that wants to become more effective in prayer and who desires to be used of God to bring transformation to a congregation and a community.

At the same time, the principles shared are flexible and adaptable. The "road map" that the Lord has revealed to Daniel over the years is adaptable to every church situation and can provide a simple and powerful strategy that can lead to authentic congregational transformation.

I believe that pastors, church leaders, and prayer leaders will not only grow in their personal prayer lives as they read and apply the principles of *Fresh Encounters*, but that they will also become better informed and equipped to motivate others to pray more consistently, powerfully, and effectively.

Daniel Henderson has a unique ability to motivate others to pray. This has been demonstrated in the lives of the people he has pastored and in the lives of many pastors and church leaders who have participated in his "Imagine What God Could Do" renewal conferences. I have had the privilege of participating in that conference and can attest to the significant contributions made to my own life and ministry.

This book is the culmination of Daniel's insights and experiences as he has been involved in our Lord's "school of prayer" over the past years. It communicates his vision for "pastor-led, local church-focused movements of Christ-exalting worship-based prayer."

I confess that I wish that this helpful book had been written a number of years ago. I believe that I could have profited greatly from it as I attempted to help the congregations that I served to become more effective in prayer.

At the same time, I am delighted that it has been written now. I recommend it to you highly. I believe it can be of great assistance to every pastor and church leader who desires to be used of God to help local churches become more effective "houses of prayer" that bring the light of Jesus Christ and true spiritual transformation to churches and communities across the nation and around the world.

—Paul Cedar
Chairman, Mission America

A Moment in His Presence

W e've heard that prayer changes things. More importantly, prayer changes us. When we are changed, and Christ's life-changing power flows powerfully in and through us, the world is changed. I warn you: Reading this book may change the world, one life at a time, starting with your own.

Changed to Be a World Changer

In October 1995, Lori gave her life to Jesus Christ. A few months later she signed up to attend a Prayer Summit sponsored by the women of our church. They were going away to pray for three days, with no agenda. This was a big stretch for a baby Christian.

At the time her song repertoire consisted of the chorus of "Amazing Grace" and "Jesus Loves Me." She writes, "I wouldn't have been able to find a book of the Bible other than Genesis if you'd paid me. And as you might imagine, I would never dream of lifting up my hands as I had seen once in one of those 'weird churches.'"

But God used that weekend to transform her life totally. She learned how to pray and worship God as the majestic, sovereign and mighty One who is worthy of praise. She saw Him take hurting people and give them peace, hope, and joy. Her life has never been the same since that weekend. How could it be the same after experiencing so dramatically the deep, deep love of Christ?

Today, Lori serves as the ministry director of a non-profit renewal organization, serving hundreds of churches around the world in the principles of worship-based prayer. God is using her in profound ways. Blessings continue to pour into her life, family, and ministry all because one day as a new believer she stepped into a praying church and was led to a life-transforming moment in His presence.

Healed and Whole

For more than a decade, Guenther and Gina lived across the street from Ken and Mary. Ken and Mary had known Christ for decades. Guenther and Gina were unchurched, expressed little interest in spiritual matters, and carried much pain from heartaches of the past.

One day, the breakthrough occurred. God opened Guenther and Gina's hearts to the gospel. They were both transformed by grace.

Soon, Ken took Guenther to some prayer events at church. A stoic, hard-driving German, Guenther was not accustomed to environments of transparency, brokenness, and tender prayer. But he could not deny what he observed with his own eyes. Scores of men, executives and blue-collar workers alike, found new connections and a fresh lease on life, as they prayed together.

Over time, Guenther opened his heart to Christ's grace as he prayed with other men. Hurts and heartaches from the past were healed and an unquenchable fire for God was kindled.

Today Guenther leads a prayer movement in his church, mobilizing men to pray for their pastors. He works on the leadership team for an annual prayer conference that reaches churches across the country. His marriage has been healed, his past cleared, and his vision ignited. He is a different man because he came to know Christ, then entered into the life of an awakened church that offered Guenther a life-changing moment in His presence.

Set Free in a Moment

Jeremy was a Christian with a dirty secret. His alcoholism was not evident to most of his friends at church, but it was slowly destroying his family, career, and health. After a family intervention Jeremy stopped drinking on the outside, but inside he was a self-described "dry alcoholic."

A few months later, at his wife's insistence, he attended a three-day men's Prayer Summit. That context of extraordinary worship, genuine acceptance, and passionate prayer exposed Jeremy's relentless addiction. He opened his heart before a group of Spirit-sensitive men. They cried out to the Lord Jesus on Jeremy's behalf. At that moment, God healed his heart, removed his addiction, and restored his life.

Today, Jeremy serves on the staff of a large West Coast church leading a dynamic ministry of small groups and recovery outreach. His wife still gets tears in her eyes when she talks about the transformation in Jeremy's life—a transformation that occurred because he experienced a profound moment with the Living Christ in a community of praying men.

Accepted and Empowered

Gloria was reeling from the pain and abandonment of a very difficult divorce. After attending a variety of divorce recovery workshops, she still struggled with deep-seated rejection and painful memories. One day Gloria was persuaded to attend a three-day women's Prayer Summit. After a couple of days of spontaneous Scripture reading and free-flowing worship, Gloria felt safe. In a tender moment, she opened her heart to the love of Jesus and the prayers of caring women. They prayed over Gloria, citing biblical truths about her true identity and acceptance in Christ. The Savior's grace touched the damaged recesses of her heart.

Since that profound encounter with Christ, Gloria has tasted and enjoyed lasting freedom. She realizes her new life in Him and experiences intimate companionship with the "friend who sticks closer than a brother" (Prov. 18:24), or husband. Every week she joins dozens of women in a dynamic Saturday morning prayer time and has emerged as a compassionate prayer leader among women. Her life is another testimony to a powerful moment in His presence.

Down but Not Out

Bob stepped into the pastor's office at his new church, his heart filled with intense anxiety. Fearing the possibility of rejection and judgment, he forced himself to share the sad details of his story.

Raised by an abusive homosexual father, Bob struggled for years to find real wholeness in Christ. At the moment, he was in the throes of a painful divorce following the departure of his wife, was embroiled in a nasty custody battle for his children and was financially bankrupt. Bob was a broken and hopeless man; but he knew this was a praying church.

Because of Christ's power unleashed in hundreds of lives, the pastor foresaw Bob's future as optimistic and hopeful. He prayed for Bob, told him he was accepted in this congregation and invited him to the church's regular prayer gatherings. During the next few years these moments in Christ's presence made a world of difference in his life.

Today, Bob is a facilitation team member at the church, leading hundreds of people into the transforming presence of Christ through a weekly prayer gathering. He has recorded a powerful CD of songs reflecting his life's story, and he travels around the country ministering through his music. His children are home, happy, flourishing, and learning to seek the Lord on a daily basis after the example of their godly father. He is "being transformed into [Christ's] likeness with ever increasing glory" (2 Cor. 3:18).

Renewal That Transcends Race

Alice and Deborah felt a strange and undeniable calling to a large church in their area. The two women are African-American. All their previous church experience was in predominantly black churches. This new congregation was almost exclusively white. During their first few months there they heard the announcement about a three-day Prayer Summit.

Alice and Deborah always felt a strong passion for prayer. Because the pastors in their previous churches did not share their burden, the impact of their prayer vision seldom found its full potential and usually was restricted to a small group of women. Since the senior pastor of the new church would lead this prayer retreat, they decided to check it out, albeit with great fear and reservation.

During the three days, God issued an unmistakable call for these women to commit to joining the "white church." Yet, the race issue still made them uncomfortable. Deborah described it like "two flies in the buttermilk." In a spontaneous, Spirit-directed moment at that Prayer Summit, the Lord resolved the issue, which began a new day for Alice and Deborah and the entire church.

At the peak of an intense time of spontaneous worship, the women began to sing a tender song. Unfortunately, no one else knew the tune well enough to join in. They sang like angels, worshiping in beautiful harmony. God used this moment to speak to the entire group. Before anyone realized what was happening, the senior pastor knelt in front of the women, hot tears running down his face. He looked them in the eyes and said, "You are welcome here."

From that day on, God has used Alice and Deborah in remarkable ways, both in and through their church. They now lead a significant prayer movement in that congregation. For more than a decade, they have taken hundreds of women away for similar Prayer Summit experiences. Deborah ministers in song at the church and at prayer events on a regular basis. Alice travels regularly teaching on the power of Christ, through prayer, to change lives and to transform a church. Alice and Deborah are unique, and have made a profound difference, because a church took time to follow the Spirit, obeying His prompting during a moment in His presence.

Lori. Guenther. Jeremy. Gloria. Bob. Alice. Deborah. Their stories have been replicated in hundreds of lives in the last decade as people have encountered God in a church that prays. These transforming experiences and inexplicable blessings are available to all who pursue a congregational lifestyle of prayer.

If you want to see your church transformed, be assured that it can happen. If you are a pastor longing for a fresh wind of inspiration in the sails of your ministry, it can happen. And, it must happen if this broken world is to experience the transforming power of Jesus through His church. The Lord is ready to bring it to pass if we will just come together and persevere in balanced, biblical prayer to enjoy a moment in His awesome presence.

This book is your invitation to join the journey toward spiritual awakening. I'm on that journey. Let's travel together and experience a fresh encounter with Christ as we learn to pray.

PART ONE

The Adventure of an Encounter

CHAPTER ONE

Fresh Encounters of a Personal Kind

M y journey of seeking Christ in prayer started during high school. God's call to full-time ministry came early. I preached my first sermon at sixteen. Knowing I was going to be a pastor, somehow, I realized I needed to pray.

In those teenage years I often tried to carve out substantive time alone, sitting in my cleared-out clothes closet or on the lonely desert hills of Southern New Mexico. It was tough, but the only way to learn to pray was by praying.

It was tough, but the only way to learn to pray was by praying.

During my college days I discovered more about the power of group prayer. For almost two years I met with some friends every weekday in a campus classroom, trying to learn to pray. Most of what I was learning was by trial and error.

My Acts 6:4 Discovery

After seminary I helped plant a church in the Pacific Northwest. In those early days I came across Acts 6:4 where it says that the early church leaders gave themselves continually to "prayer and the ministry of the word." I tried to understand what it meant for a pastor to be fully engaged in the prayer ministry and lead people into this extraordinary reality.

At that time, I began leading daily early-morning prayer, all-night prayer, and days of prayer. By God's grace that commitment has been sustained. I've known the joy of leading multiple prayer times every week for almost 25 years. Of course, my motives and methods matured significantly over the decades. Yet my vision and passion continue to grow as the sense of real awakening increases in my heart.

> *Prayer is the most-often talked about,*
> *but the least practiced discipline in the Christian life.*

I'm on a journey to a genuine, prayer-fueled awakening, not only in me, but also in Christ's church. Even though prayer is the most-often talked about, but the least practiced discipline in the Christian life, we must persist in the pathway and experience all God has for us.

The Local Church Laboratory of Desperate Prayer

My continuing passion for prayer has been forged in the laboratory of local church ministry. Each of my primary pastoral assignments has been uniquely challenging, which is probably what has driven me to my knees.

My first assignment involved a church in California in rapid decline as it faced a $25 million lawsuit and a moral failure by the previous senior pastor. The second took me to a very traditional church in Sacramento after its beloved founding pastor, who had led the church for 40 years, retired. The third assignment led me to a megachurch in Minnesota that had just built a 4,500-seat auditorium and took on an $18 million mortgage, but fell short an additional $10 million in its capital cash campaign. On top of this, six weeks after this church moved to its new campus the public learned the pastor was having an affair.

A friend told me he was going to write a book about my pastoral journey and call it *Dumb, Dumber, and Dumberer*. In all seriousness, those three assignments were excruciating, but in each congregation God had placed wonderful people who were willing to pray and trust Him for healing and wholeness. I fell in love with each church and was glad the Lord could use me to help and call the people afresh into His powerful, restoring presence. I learned most of what I know about prayer on my knees with the extraordinary people in all three churches.

The First Challenge
I was only 30 years old when God called me to the first challenging assignment at a large church in the San Francisco Bay area where I followed a pastor who had a 28-year tenure. Under his leadership the church grew from 60 people to more than 6,000. Unfortunately, in June 1988 he announced his resignation due to the disclosure of an affair that had occurred years earlier. The church also was embroiled in a large lawsuit over a church discipline dispute.

When I arrived I had no idea how difficult it would be. I stayed for four years, during which time God gave us many extraordinary experiences of His healing grace though all-night prayer meetings, hundreds of early-morning prayer gatherings, and intense expressions of intercession during services and outreach events. During this season, the Lord broke me dramatically with painful wounds that now have become empowering scars. I often joke that I was at this church as long as my predecessor because four years in "dog years" equals 28.

An Older Church Prays in New Ways
I then went to Arcade Church in Sacramento. Arcade was planted as a new work in a growing suburb in 1950. The congregation saw some years of early growth as the city expanded and engulfed the neighborhoods surrounding the church. As it often happens, the ministry hit a plateau with nearly 1,100 people in attendance 15 years prior to my arrival. I inherited a completely built-out campus on only seven acres. The surrounding area stagnated with no

new housing developments within miles of the church, which then was $2.7 million in debt.

I followed an exceptional, godly pastor who had served faithfully. Of course, succeeding a beloved leader is usually a high-risk assignment, but God had great plans. I arrived with a clear vision of a prayer-energized renewal. During my first month in town I began training others to help lead effective prayer meetings. Much of what you will read in this book comprised the core of what I taught. Soon we started several strategic weekly prayer gatherings. I also preached a fervent and practical series on prayer.

Six months later we hosted our first all-church Prayer Summit, a three-day retreat with no sermons and no agenda—just high expectations. When I announced the summit, I hoped for 30 people to attend, realizing this unique format required great sacrifice for people to attend from Wednesday evening to Saturday afternoon.

Ninety people answered the call. For three days we engaged in spontaneous Scripture reading, worship, and responsive prayer. We celebrated the Lord's Table twice and spent significant times in small groups. It was the closest to genuine revival I have ever experienced. God transformed many lives as hearts were healed, marriages were restored, and personal devotion to Christ was fanned. Dozens were set free from habitual sin. A movement of renewal began that eventually took our church through the incredible rollercoaster ride of congregational change.

During my 11 years at Arcade we hosted more than 30 such Prayer Summits, attracting groups between 80 and 225 people. We sponsored approximately 13 prayer meetings weekly, the largest being our Thursday evening Fresh Encounters service with 200 to 400 in attendance. More than 100 people served as Pastor's Prayer Partners.

We organized an active World Prayer Center where people came to pray an hour once a week. Over a span of five years we hosted an annual prayer conference to equip other church leaders in local church prayer ministries. Each conference attracted nearly 500 attendees from 14 states, several foreign countries, and

19 denominations. A real awakening was occurring, and the only explanation was Christ's true, biblical prayer recipe.

Tangible Fruit

On the surface we saw the fruit of ministry expansion. Our weekly attendance and annual budget almost doubled. Our missions giving grew substantially. Multiplied dozens went to the mission field for short-term experiences or full-time careers. We also planted several daughter churches.

The spirit of the church was transformed. When I first arrived, the phrase I often heard was "We've never done it that way before." Later our ministry was marked by the slogan, "We're going to do something a little different today." A profound spirit of prayer and expectation emerged. Many young families and new Christians became vitally involved in the church.

Seasoned older saints joined the frontlines of our ministry. One pastor friend of mine from New York visited our congregation a few times. His observation said it well: "Daniel, your church has the youngest old people I have ever seen in my life." That is what spiritual awakening produces.

Dependence through Difficulty

My third assignment was undoubtedly the most difficult. I had no reason to leave Sacramento except that God clearly gave our family His marching orders to go and try to bring healing and spiritual restoration to a church that was on the brink of disaster.

Grace Church of Eden Prairie, Minnesota, has a profound and fruitful history of local and global ministry. After raising $25 million in cash to relocate, the church's plans were interrupted by 9/11 and the "dot com" crisis. The $18 million mortgage was overwhelming enough, but a $10 million shortfall was nothing less than ominous. When the church lost its pastor immediately after moving due to marital infidelity, the situation became fragile.

Yet God birthed a wonderful work of renewal through weekly Fresh Encounter prayer services, three Prayer Summits a year, and a variety of other faithful prayer gatherings, including hosting several national prayer conferences. The church literally rose from the ashes of tragic disappointment while on its knees.

I am now a missionary of Grace Church. The elders and congregation, along with the board of directors of my renewal ministry (www.strategicrenewal.com), all sensed the Lord launching me full-time into a ministry of igniting the heart of the church through efforts of personal renewal, congregational revival, and leadership restoration. I say I have gone from being a senior pastor to becoming a "spiritual pyromaniac."

I have the joy of returning to all three of my former congregations fairly regularly to preach, lead prayer events, and celebrate the victories we all enjoyed as we sought the Lord together. As I write this, I have just completed the most meaningful three-day Prayer Summit of my life at Grace Church. The Lord is continuing the work He began in powerful and fruitful ways.

Current Models, Future Movements

My passion for prayer keeps me in the local church. After 25 years of full-time pastoral ministry, I now serve part-time as Pastor of Renewal at the 12,000-member Thomas Road Baptist Church in central Virginia. The church is in the midst of the early "mercy drops" of revival. In the last year more than 1,000 people have been baptized; hundreds more have been saved and are joining the church. Senior Pastor Jonathan Falwell is hungry to seek the Lord and lead the church into new heights of prayer.

I also have the opportunity to teach and lead prayer events at nearby Liberty University, where a living laboratory of more than 10,000 campus students allows me to train a new generation. The Lord is fuelling many unique movements of prayer among the students. We are calling them away to Prayer Summits, taking them to see places like Brooklyn Tabernacle's Tuesday night prayer meeting, equipping them with prayer tools, and seeking to launch them out to ignite fresh movements of prayer.

My unique passion is to see God develop models of prayer-based congregations and revived churches. My heart is to encourage and equip pastors to lead their people into these new spiritual heights. Only Christ-centered prayer movements will awaken churches as passionate pastors who depend on God lead congregations. If pastors mobilize their people to pray, the world will be transformed.

As a result of reading this book, I pray you will:

- Become impassioned with a vision for a true spiritual awakening in your life, church, family, and society.
- Learn biblical and practical approaches to corporate prayer that will enable you to be more influential in prayer.
- Identify a broad range of corporate prayer opportunities, and be encouraged to commit to lead the way.
- Receive practical instruction on the vision, dedication, and skills necessary to sustain a long-term movement of life-changing prayer.
- Experience and exhibit the manifest glory of Christ in His church.

"I would rather teach one man to pray than ten to preach."

The Fire of a Fresh Encounter

I pray for the day the church will arise with undeniable supernatural impact that can only be explained by Christ's glory in the midst of His praying people.

Andrew Murray once wrote, "The man who mobilized the Christian church to prayer will make the greatest contribution to world evangelization in history."[1] By the grace of God, and with a passion for His glory, I believe you could be that man or woman. Your church could be a beginning point of a genuine work of revival. My prayer is that God will ignite a fire in your soul that will lead many into a fresh encounter with the living Christ.

Charles Spurgeon, the "Prince of Preachers," stated: "I would rather teach one man to pray than ten men to preach."[2] Perhaps God is calling you to embrace this as your goal. If so, this book is for you. If you're not sure yet, keep reading. You never know what God might want to do in and through you.

No matter where you are or what kind of church you serve, an awakening—a fresh encounter—can occur through the power for prayer. Too often we try to reorganize the church to health. We create new slogans, mottos, and mission statements. We initiate cutting-edge programs to reach the lost, attract the youth and impact the community. But we lack the fire of a fresh encounter.

This book is not a call to newer or better programs. It is a map for the pathway to real spiritual awakening in your life and church. A life-changing fresh encounter is just around the corner. Let's journey there—together.

Endnotes

1. Ivan French. *The IFCA Voice*, Sept. 2, 2003.
2. Charles Spurgeon. From *Turning Point Daily Devotional*, Feb. 17, 2004 (San Diego: Turning Point Ministries).

CHAPTER TWO

Your Call to an Encounter

"*D*aniel, you could be stranded on a desert island for a week without once noticing that no one else is around," my wife once observed.

Admittedly, this is a slight overstatement, but my personality is fiercely independent and self-sufficient. I am a driven, task-oriented, and entrepreneurial leader. Prayer involves humility, depending on God rather than self, and finding our sufficiency in Christ. The bottom line: I am not a natural "prayer guy."

Have you ever met one of those "prayer types"? They seem to glow with the glory of God and can spend hours a day in prayer. They write lofty, inspiring books about realities most of us have never tasted. I praise the Lord for these amazing saints.

But that's not me. I am not a "contemplative" personality. Prayer is hard work. All the Lord taught me and I practiced came through the school of hard knocks and sore knees.

The good news is that if I can learn how to practice biblical, balanced prayer, I know you can too. If you are interested in a life-long passion for God, this book can help you. If you want to see your church become a powerful, praying church—you're holding a tool right now that can get you there.

My passion in ministry is pastor-led, local church-focused movements of worship-based prayer. *Fresh Encounters* is designed to challenge pastors and church leaders. But, if you are not a pastor or leader—but simply a person interested in prayer—it is for you, too. You will learn how to encourage and pray for your pastor and church leadership. You'll learn about and catch a vision for a biblical and life-transforming approach, called worship-based prayer. As you change in His presence, you can become a change agent for others in encountering the living Christ.

> *My passion in ministry is pastor-led, local church-oriented movements of Christ-exalting, worship-based prayer — leading to a full-scale revival, supernatural evangelism and cultural transformation.*

Tom's Discovery

Tom Norris' story is a real-life story of hope. Tom, a missionary to inner-city Los Angeles, discovered the life-transforming power of worship-based prayer. Not long ago, he and his wife visited our church's daily staff prayer meeting while attending our missions conference. Since that time everything has changed.

He says, "Our ministry staff prayer meetings in Los Angeles were based on prayer requests. Bored, I looked at my watch wondering when the meetings would end. But here the prayer time was so good and refreshing. At the end I looked at my watch and thought, *I can't believe it. An hour went by.* My wife and I discussed taking this new type of prayer meeting back to Los Angeles."

Missionaries at the conference received a CD set about how to teach their churches to pray. (This book is based on those principles.) "I thought I could use this to pass on to others," Tom noted.

One way Tom applied the principles was through a summer mission's project he directs in Los Angeles. Thirty-five to forty college students and about twelve staff members came. He relates, "I announced the theme for the project: Prayer. I got blank looks.

They'd all been to boring prayer meetings."

"The next morning I began teaching on prayer, condensing the information down to two meetings. We prayed afterwards for an hour or an hour and a half.

"The students became excited and began getting a vision for it. During the evaluation one student wrote: 'When I heard prayer was the theme, I wasn't excited. Then I saw how uplifting and even fun it can be.'

"When I asked the students, 'what was the highlight of the week?,' the most common answer was prayer. They never experienced worship-based prayer before. It was intimate, especially in a corporate setting."

A few mornings that week the students arose at 6 a.m. to pray. Their attendance was optional. Between fifteen and twenty students came even though they were busy from 7 a.m. until 9 or 10 p.m. During the previous years the prayer meetings (without worship-based prayer) brought one or two students to pray for requests.

Tom's boss heard about the summer project. Tom is now leading an enthusiastic revival of prayer in their thirty-member staff meetings. In addition, he has been asked to work with 300 inner-city churches using the principles in this book.

What is worship-based prayer? Worship-based prayer begins with and is fueled by God and His character, not our needs. It is a prayer meeting where singing, spontaneous Scripture reading and prayers that focus on who God is flow freely.

> *Worship-based prayer begins with and is fueled by God and His character, not our needs.*

This approach is also making a big difference at Tom's church. "I gave the information to our assistant pastor. He listened to it and loved it. Then he did the same for our senior pastor. Now the church has worship-based prayer each Tuesday and Thursday. People quickly catch a vision for it. The material is so transferable and easy to teach to others."

Personal Impact

Tom's personal prayer life also has been impacted. He says, "When we go to the Lord in prayer, it is always refreshing and intimate. God is good. The asking part is easy because I feel connected to the Lord. I'm requesting the right things. The Bible says to ask whatever is His will, and it will be done for you. I know His will. I'm more in tune with it and the people around me.

"I used to ask for things when I needed them. Now I'm more inclined to start off praising the Lord. My wife and I pray together, singing, listening to a musical CD, or reading a psalm. We wait a significant amount of time before we ask for anything. My heart attitude changed. I'm much more thankful. It's easier to pray because it's more of a lifestyle."

This is how the Holy Spirit helps people pray. This book is a plea for a true spiritual revival and awakening—an awakening birthed on our knees. The awakening began in my heart. Without that I would not have the courage or conviction to write this. I suppose the awakening burns in your heart also since you are reading this book now.

Experiencing His Presence

When the church becomes a house of prayer, the glory (manifest presence) of Christ is evidenced and effective. One of my greatest joys as a pastor has been to interact with dozens of people who visit our church for the first time. Again and again they caught me in the lobby, often with tears in their eyes, saying, "The presence of God is in this place." This meant more to me than any praise about the sermon, compliment on the music or rave review about the high-tech Sunday program. This reality in our church was the direct fruit of a prayer movement and dawn of a spiritual awakening.

Paul describes our experience of Jesus' glory in these words:

But we all, with unveiled face beholding as in a mirror the glory of the Lord, are being transformed into the same

image from glory to glory, just as from the Lord, the Spirit.
. . . Therefore, since we have this ministry, as we received
mercy, we do not lose heart. (2 Cor. 3:18, 4:1 NASB)

While we often view this as an individual experience, it is entirely appropriate to see this as a corporate reality in the church. When our ministry is a passionate, life-transforming engagement of Jesus' glory, it is marked by supernatural impact and fueled with spiritual endurance.

The source of our impact becomes clear as Paul goes on to say:

For God, who said, "Light shall shine out of darkness," is
the One who has shone in our hearts to give the light of
the knowledge of the glory of God in the face of Christ.
But we have this treasure in earthen vessels, so that the
surpassing greatness of the power may be of God and not
from ourselves. (2 Cor. 4:6-7, NASB)

Compare this with Paul's comment about the real effect of God's presence on the unbeliever: "The secrets of his heart are disclosed; and so he will fall on his face and worship God, declaring that God is certainly among you" (1 Cor. 14:25, NASB).

Attraction or Influence?

In our efforts to attract and impress lost people with our clever tactics and high-octane programs perhaps we forget to influence them through Christ's noticeable presence in the midst of His church.

> *If pastors would mobilize their people*
> *to pray, the world would be transformed.*

Coaxed by his girlfriend, a young man who was studying for the priesthood came to our church one Sunday. With misconceptions about attending a Protestant church, he drew back until she nudged him toward the door. That day someone led him to accept Christ. Later at his baptism he said, "The minute I walked in the door it was as if God's presence pulled me into this church."

All this happens as a result of a praying church, a church that seeks God together, through corporate prayer. The early days of the church were dominated by corporate prayer (see Acts 1, 2). And God transformed the world at that time through a praying church. The same could happen today. If pastors would mobilize their people to pray by the grace of Christ and for the glory of Christ, the world would be transformed.

Countless thousands in our communities are wandering in a spiritual wilderness, looking for something real and transforming. Thousands of others are rummaging in the wasteland of dead religion waiting to be pulled into a life-changing encounter with the living Christ through His church. For their sake, we must pursue a new level of prayer and spiritual power. The journey will not be easy. It is an uphill battle in our self-sufficient, highly programmed culture. We must be honest about the challenges but resolute. It will be worth it.

CHAPTER THREE

The Predicament of the Empty Prayer Room

*L*et's be honest from the start. Leading your church to an awakening is not going to be easy. I suspect the current prayer level of your congregation is underwhelming. For the most part, prayer meetings are sparse, attendance is sporadic and the inertia is obvious to all. If we are going to see things change we must identify the common obstacles and prepare our hearts to overcome these barriers to a fresh encounter with Christ through a new kind of prayer leadership.

Of Course I Pray!

For many years Bob and Joyce Bridges were complacent about prayer meetings at church. Weekly announcements of the midweek intercessor's gathering stimulated a dutiful, artificial nod but little resolve. Over the years, they sporadically sampled these prayer times but Bob decided he would rather stay home to watch sitcoms or CNN.

After a long battle with cancer, Bob went home to the Lord. Yet, his joy and victory during his final years were contagious.

For the most part, he credited his spiritual vitality to the transforming power of Christ, experienced through corporate prayer.

The change started over a decade ago when Joyce attended her first three-day Prayer Summit, sponsored by our church. In thirty years as a Christian, she was never so rekindled in her love for Jesus and passion to seek Him. When the annual men's Prayer Summit rolled around a few months later, she "nagged Bob" (her words) until he agreed to go. At that Summit, Bob was restored to his first love, delivered from some destructive life-long habits, and radically renewed in his romance with Joyce.

Their lives have truly never been the same. They enjoy and even lead weekly prayer meetings. When the doctor delivered the news of Bob's cancer, they felt prepared for the trial.

Bob and Joyce's experience of the power of corporate prayer is fairly rare in today's culture. Like many, Joyce did not initially think she needed this kind of renewal. She admits that when she first heard me talk about prayer from the pulpit she whispered under her breath, "He sure has nerve talking like that. Of course I pray!" Joyce's experience had been limited to private, request-based prayer. Now, her whole approach to prayer, privately and corporately, has changed. Most importantly, both their lives have changed.

Overcoming the Resistance to Corporate Prayer

In the average church only a motivated minority regularly participates in the congregational prayer times. This reality has discouraged many a pastor and prayer leader. Most have given up trying to develop powerful united prayer. But it doesn't have to be that way. What would it take for the average Christian to find greater reward in praying with other believers? How can corporate prayer be transformed from an obligation to an oasis?

> *How can corporate prayer be transformed*
> *from an obligation to an oasis?*

If we want to overcome this resistance to corporate prayer, we need first to consider what keeps people from wanting to pray together. Based on practical experience and key principles from God's Word, I have identified six basic reasons people resist the call to prayer and stay away from church prayer gatherings. If we are to lead an awakening of prayer, we must understand and overcome these objections.

Independence from God

I often state, "Prayerlessness is my declaration of independence from God." At heart, prayer is depending on God. Many of us in today's high-tech world of creature comforts and great abundance have a hard time stopping our frenetic activity to simply focus on God. Jesus reminded us, "Remain in me, and I will remain in you. No branch can bear fruit by itself; it must remain in the vine. Neither can you bear fruit unless you remain in me" (Jn. 15:4).

> *Prayerlessness is my declaration of independence from God.*

In spite of this essential and familiar truth, we still think we can do things on our own. When this core attitude is multiplied by dozens, hundreds, or even thousands of church members, it results in busy Christians but empty prayer meetings. Because it is so easy to "succeed" in church work these days we tend to forget that we are ultimately called to a supernatural task.

Let me illustrate. If I asked you to take my car keys and move my Toyota 4-Runner from the back parking lot to the front parking lot of the building, you would probably be willing to oblige. On the other hand, if I asked you to fly my 747 jumbo jet from Minneapolis to Miami, you would break out in a cold sweat. (By the way, I do not have a 747).

You see, moving the Toyota is a task you can easily accomplish. Flying a jumbo jet is probably far beyond your skills. Sadly, we've come to the conclusion that living the Christian life is more like moving the car than flying the 747. Nothing could actually be farther from the truth. Jesus said that if we fail to abide in Him we can do nothing of eternal significance and lasting fruitfulness. Because we think we can live the Christian life, we conclude that we do not need to pray.

One goal of this book is to help you overcome the spiritual inertia so prevalent in our churches while stimulating a fresh sense of spiritual neediness. Most importantly, you will be challenged to lead the way by your own example of depending on God with a heart of true dependence.

B-O-R-I-N-G

Unfortunately, prayer meetings can be and have often been very boring. They often lack fervor and focus. Why? Is Jesus dull? Is time in His presence intentioned to be one step above a night of C-SPAN? No, the problem is not God. It is our approach to prayer.

Fresh Encounters examines a specific and dynamic pattern for our prayer times. We will take a fresh look at it in detail later. According to this plan, prayer should always commence with worship (*"Our Father in heaven, hallowed be your name"* [Mt. 6:9]). God-centered worship then leads to concentrated surrender. (*"Your kingdom come, your will be done on earth as it is in heaven"* [Mt. 6:10]). This surrender is essentially a yieldedness to the Holy Spirit who leads us into the will of God (Rom. 8:27) and empowers us to be fruitful for the kingdom of God (Jn. 16:13-14; Gal. 5:23-24).

In contrast, many of today's prayer meetings are based on inter-personal sharing of requests. As a result, the majority of the activity tends to eclipse God's design for Spirit-inspired corporate prayer. The enjoyment of His glorious presence slips the footnotes.

Often, prayer meetings encompass extended casual conversations between participants, scattered Bible discussion, extended moaning and groaning ("prayer requests") and, if time permits, a few minutes telling God about our problems. Don't get me wrong. There is a place for prayer requests: a special prayer group, prayer chain, perhaps a needs list each week in the bulletin, maybe in small groups. But churches need to learn that our most effective prayers spring from a base of worship.

In a corporate prayer setting, the request-focused model tends to go flat fast. We all know what it is like when the group begins to pray for all the noted needs—then runs out of gas. There are periods of long silence. Participants become uncomfortable and start drumming up things to pray about just to keep everyone from falling asleep. God must grieve over this gross under-enjoyment of time in His presence.

This is often the impression people have of corporate prayer meetings. No wonder our announcements about prayer fall on deaf ears. We need a new model; our churches need a different paradigm.

Fresh Encounters will introduce you to a different model. You will learn to practice and implement what we will call "worship-based" prayer. You will discover that a gathering of this kind is as solid, broad, and exciting as the character of God. The prayer time is no longer a grocery list of our problems but a celebration of our problem solver.

Concerns about Gossip

Not long ago I enjoyed lunch with one of America's best-known pastors. As we discussed various aspects of his multifaceted and prominent church, I asked about their prayer meetings. He stated, "Oh, we have a few women who gather every once in a while, but we are trying to shut it down because it is nothing more than a gossip session." Over the years I have learned that many dedicated church members carry the same suspicion when it comes to corporate prayer.

This is another danger of a request-based approach. The typical mode of sitting around "sharing" the trials and traumas of people in the church can easily downgrade to inappropriate chit-chat. Sometimes the devil is in the details.

We are going to learn that a strong worship-based prayer time tends to eliminate the loose lips syndrome. A genuine and extended focus on the character of God calls every participant to a serious accountability in His presence. Unnecessary and unkind speech stands out like a sore thumb in this context.

Another dynamic occurs in the initial season of worship. Everyone is reminded that God is all-knowing, gracious, and sufficient for every need. The compulsion to share juicy details is minimized, as each participant trusts Him with every situation—spoken and unspoken. You will learn to lead prayer times that transcend the tendency to gossip.

Fear of Praying Aloud in Public

Gloria Ho was born in Shanghai, China. She moved to the United States as a young adult. Shy by nature and insecure with a new language, Gloria seldom spoke in groups and certainly was uncomfortable praying in front of others. On those occasions when she did attend a prayer time, she was quite intimidated by the beautiful, flowing intercessions of seasoned saints.

In recent years Gloria has found great freedom at prayer meetings. She now attends weekly prayer times at her church and frequently verbalizes her prayers. She has even shared public testimonies about her newfound love for the presence of Jesus.

I am a talkative extrovert so it is hard for me to relate to the fear of praying aloud. But the fact remains that many, like Gloria, stay away from prayer times for years (some for life) because they are uncomfortable praying aloud in the presence of others. But in time, and by grace, a breakthrough can occur even for the very shy and intimidated.

As you lead in prayer you will discover the natural tension that often exists between the verbose veterans and the more introverted, intimidated newcomers. Sadly, we have often evaluated someone's intimacy with God and power in prayer by the way they put together pithy and passionate sentences.

As you learn to lead in prayer it is important to remember that God does not see it that way. He looks at the heart. Our Father does not evaluate your time with Him by the volume or velocity of your speech. But He does delight when we join other members of His family to enjoy His presence.

You are going to learn how to encourage introverts (and extroverts) to pray from the Scriptures. The Bible has a powerful way of giving speech to needy hearts, even for those who do not naturally have a personality given to wordiness. Often a brief prayer framed from the Bible means more than the man-made verbal onslaught we often classify as prevailing prayer. It is better for the heart to be without words than the words without heart. You can teach people to pray accordingly.

Nominal Attendance by Others in the Church

It is common to initiate a prayer meeting only to be let down by meager participation. This can be discouraging and provides the perfect excuse to give up the fight.

For years I have been disheartened with the sparse turnout at prayer meetings. I've heard it said, "Don't expect a big crowd when God is the only attraction." This statement reflects our concern—and our answer.

The pattern and practice of worship-based prayer eventually will attract more participants. More importantly, it will provide an enduring motive and engaging method that will keep the focus where it belongs. God is the attraction, not the size of the crowd.

Lack of Understanding of the Importance of Corporate Prayer

In our culture of rugged individualism we have come to the conclusion that it is better to pray alone than with others. Unfortunately, most of us never learn to do either one very well. Like most disciplines of the Christian faith, we learn best to pray alone when we have been taught in community. The believers in Acts experienced a balanced diet of corporate spirituality as they engaged in "the apostles teaching and to the fellowship and to the breaking of bread and to prayer" (Acts 2:42). Obviously, prayer was one of the vital components of their corporate experience and personal learning. We need to create a new sense of community in prayer to help people rise above their individualistic bent.

Making a Comeback

The thought of going back to corporate prayer times may not feel very compelling to those you will lead. Yet, I would urge you to understand and work through the obstacles that keep them away. As you teach the principles of prayer, lead with faithfulness and persevere with conviction. Lives *will* be changed and a movement *will* occur.

We all know that congregational prayer is too important to be relegated to a rut of unattractive routine. Praying with others is too central to a balanced faith and a revived church to be left on the back shelf of excuses. We must try again, asking God for a new vision to make prayer times better and more attractive to others who have been turned off.

Renewed in Returning

Connie Acker grew up in a pastor's home. In her youth she clocked many hours at midweek prayer meetings, like it or not. For her it was usually "not." As an adult, her attraction to prayer meetings was minimal. She had better, more exciting things to do.

Still, she struggled to learn prayer on her own. Her pattern of private, request-based prayer left her flat. One day she discovered the difference of a worship-based approach while attending a corporate prayer gathering. For the first time, she realized her prayers could be based in praise and given language from the Bible. Not only did she become a regular attendee, but now she administrates one of the largest local church prayer ministries in the nation.

At first it was hard for Connie to return to corporate prayer. Now, as she recruits others, she understands the fears and barriers so many experience. She has become living proof that it is worth it to overcome these obstacles. Connie has rediscovered the blessing of praying with others and, by her own admission, her life will never be the same.

How many just like Connie are sitting in your church today, waiting for a new challenge and a fresh vision? How many are living in the dull twilight of discouragement, embracing a variety of excuses that could be easily overcome by clear teaching and passionate leadership? Only the Lord knows. The Lord also knows, and has made it clear to us, that living with those excuses is unacceptable. May you become His agent for change as you issue a compelling call to a fresh encounter in His presence.

CHAPTER FOUR

Where's Jesus?

A favorite childhood cartoon, "The Flintstones," captured my imagination with their ever-exciting lives in Bedrock. I loved the closing seconds of the introduction to the show. Fred puts Dino, their comical pet dinosaur, outside for the night. Then he places the milk bottles on the front porch without noticing Dino jumping in the window and locking Fred outside. The scene closes with Fred knocking on the door of his house, frantically yelling "Wilma! Wilma!" As a kid, I always found it hilarious to see Fred locked out of his house, unable to get inside.

The glorified Christ told a similar story in Revelation 3 as He spoke to the church in Laodicea about their spiritual condition. Only, it was not so funny.

> I know your deeds, that you are neither cold nor hot. I wish you were either one or the other! So, because you are lukewarm—neither hot nor cold—I am about to spit you out of my mouth. You say, "I am rich; I have acquired wealth and do not need a thing." But you do not realize that you are wretched, pitiful, poor, blind and naked. I counsel you to buy from me gold refined in the fire, so you

can become rich; and white clothes to wear, so you can cover your shameful nakedness; and salve to put on your eyes, so you can see. Those whom I love I rebuke and discipline. So be earnest, and repent. Here I am! I stand at the door and knock. If anyone hears my voice and opens the door, I will come in and eat with him, and he with me. To him who overcomes, I will give the right to sit with me on my throne, just as I overcame and sat down with my Father on his throne. He who has an ear, let him hear what the Spirit says to the churches. (3:15-22)

They thought of themselves as "rich, [having] acquired wealth and [did] not need a thing" (v. 17). The Lord saw it differently. He told them they were "wretched, pitiful, poor, blind and naked" (v. 17) and in need of a spiritual revival. Their problem: Jesus was on the outside looking inside. He stood at the door of the worship gathering knocking. If they would recognize their need, turn from spiritual indifference and open the door, He was eager to enter, renew their lukewarm hearts and restore them to intimate fellowship.

I've often wondered how Jesus landed outside this church. Some say the church was unregenerate and He never was inside to start with. But I do not think He would call it a "church" of people He loved if this was the case. Rather, I think their self-sufficiency, pride, and superficial activity shoved His presence from the center of attention to the back porch.

The scary component in this commentary was the denial of their true condition, their failure to realize that Jesus was no longer gloriously present among them. Could the same thing happen to a prayer-deprived church today?

Where's Jesus?

We remember the creative brainteaser books called *Where's Waldo?* This distinctive fellow, dressed in colorful clothes, caused readers to scour page after page of busy scenes looking for Waldo amid the crowds. It was quite the rage.

As we look across the landscape of congregations in our land, it is good to ask the question: "Where's Jesus?" Is He in the middle of everything that happens, somewhere in a remote corner, or standing in the parking lot?

Most students of culture conclude that the United States is post-Christian. That bothers us, so we try harder. We have more conferences on church programming, seminars on evangelism, and books on leadership than any Christian society in history. We enjoy unprecedented affluence, state-of-the-art technology, and the finest in Christian education through an abundance of colleges and seminaries. But where's Jesus?

Borrowing from Jim Cymbala, I often explain that we can tell how popular the preacher is by who comes on Sunday mornings. We can tell how popular the church is by how many people are involved in the midweek programs. We can tell how popular Jesus is by who attends the prayer meetings. So, where is Jesus?

In this day of need-based, consumer-driven ministry we have displaced the centrality and supremacy of Christ. We are attracting people to spiritual centers of Christian concern to find a superficial healing rather than bringing hearts into the holy presence of Christ, who is the sole source of a transformed life. The preaching of Christ, the worship of His glorious name in song, and the central place of His sufficiency in our prayers have quietly slid off the radar screen of popular ministry.

Trying Harder—Achieving Less

Regardless of the feeling many of us have that "status quo" is working just fine, objective research indicates that we need an infusion of supernatural grace to increase our impact on society. For example:

- Five hundred billion dollars has been spent on ministry in the United States in the last fifteen years with no appreciable growth in the impact of the church.[1]
- During the last ten years the combined membership of all Protestant denominations has decreased 9.5 percent while the national population has increased 11.4 percent.[2]

- In recent years, half of all churches did not add one new member through conversion growth.[3]

Other data reveals that some eighty-five percent of all churches are on a plateau or in decline. Only one percent are growing as a result of new conversions. This means the remaining fourteen percent are growing only through transfers from the declining majority of congregations.[4]

Estimates tell us that every month as many as 2,700 churches in the Unites States alone hold their last service, close their doors, and put up the "For Sale" sign.[5] In a telling summary of his findings researcher George Barna offers these concerns:

> It's a bit troubling to see pastors feel they're doing a great job when the research reveals that few congregants have a biblical worldview, half the people they minister to are not spiritually secure or developed, kids are fleeing from the church in record numbers, most of the people who attend worship service admit they did not connect with God, the divorce rate among Christians is not different than that of non-Christians, only 2% of the pastors themselves can identify God's vision for their ministry they are trying to lead, and the average congregant spends more time watching television in one day than he spends in all spiritual pursuits combined for an entire week.[6]

Still, two-thirds of pastors agree strongly that spiritual revival is the single most pressing issue facing the church in America today. I would agree.

Two-thirds of pastors agree strongly that spiritual revival is the single most pressing issue facing the church in America today.

So where is Jesus and what are we doing to give Him the front-and-center role in our gatherings? Of course, I cannot answer that, but some other statistics challenge me to think deeply about our condition.

Working Harder—Praying Less?

For instance, research by Peter Wagner indicates that the average pastor in America spends less than thirty minutes a day in prayer. Other recent research from Bruce Demarest, a Denver Seminary professor, states that the average Christian spends five minutes a day in prayer and that the average pastor spends only seven minutes.[7] Jonathan Graf, editor of *Pray!* magazine, notes that, at best, five percent of churches have a significant mobilized prayer ministry.

> *There is a difference whether we use all of these tools or depend on them. The acid test is the prayer level of the church.*

I am not against education, technology, evangelism programs, and excellent Sunday worship. I have acquired advanced degrees in my educational pursuits. My church uses state-of-the-art equipment, enjoys a large and beautiful facility, and implements a truckload of programs.

But there is a difference whether we *use* all of these tools or *depend* on them. The acid test is the prayer level of the church. Churches lacking extraordinary prayer depend on the tools, leaving Jesus on the periphery. Praying churches are free to use or discard the tools. Their one concern is to keep Jesus where He belongs—at the center of everything, giving Him significant amounts of undivided attention on their knees.

I am convicted but inspired by E. M. Bounds' timeless words:

It is better to let the work go by default than to let the praying go by neglect. Whatever affects the intensity of our praying affects the value of our work. "Too busy to pray" is not only the keynote to backsliding, but it mars even the work done. Nothing is well done without prayer for the simple reason that it leaves God out of the account. It is so easy to be seduced by the good to neglect the best, until both the good and the best perish. How easy to neglect prayer or abbreviate our praying simply by the plea that we have church work on our hands. Satan has effectively disarmed us when he can keep us too busy doing things to stop and pray.[8]

A Simple Sailboat

In my high-school years I lived on a lake. During those years I enjoyed many days of boating and skiing. I loved to take our old outboard and speed across the lake with the wind in my face, blowing my hair (back when I had hair!).

Perhaps that is why one day my heart was gripped as I flew from California to Pennsylvania to speak at a pastor's conference. I will never forget being in that crowded airplane looking out the window with tears streaming down my face. I had just finished reading a book on leadership and was reflecting honestly about my journey in ministry. I confessed:

> Lord, for so many years I've wanted to be a powerboat for you. As a pastor, I've kept my hand on the throttle of a man-made machine, enjoying the exhilaration of impressive speed. I've sliced through the choppy waters of church life impressing people with my dynamic ability to navigate and steer.

I continued with a broken heart: "Please give me the grace to learn to be a simple sailboat. Let this be the true attitude of my heart. Let me set my sails everyday through prayer and the Word and wait for the wind of Your Spirit to blow."

I learned that a powerboat is impressive, but its mark of distinction is human creativity and effort. A simple sailboat is average and only able to move by an unseen supernatural force. A powerboat advances on a predictable journey at the hands of the driver, propelled by man-made fuel. A sailboat is at the mercy of an unpredictable force and magnifies the beauty and energy of the wind.

This illustration represents two different approaches to life and ministry. At the center of our consideration is the issue of genuine, passionate, and enduring Christ-centered prayer.

I remember hearing Pastor Jim Cymbala say that he did not want to stand before Christ someday and say to the Lord, "Look what I did for you!" Instead he longed to fall on his face and cry, "Thank you for what You did through me."

We need to resolve to be simple sailboats. Apart from the Spirit of God's moving, we are dead in the water. When the Spirit moves, our only goal is to bring glory to the unseen Force that propels our lives. Perhaps then people will cry out, "There's Jesus! Right where He belongs—glorious among His people."

Endnotes

1. Barna Research Group, "The State of the Church 2002," June 4, 2004.
2. United States Census statistic for 1990 and 1999; *Yearbook of American & Canadian Churches* (Nashville: Abingdon Press, 1990 & 1999).
3. Barna Research Group, "America's Congregations: More Money But Fewer People," December 6, 1999.
4. George Barna, *Inward, Outward & Upward: Ministry That Transforms Lives* (Ventura, CA: Barna Research Group, Ltd., 1999), pp. 5-6.
5. Charles Arn, *How to Start a New Service* (Grand Rapids: Baker Books, 1997), p. 16.
6. Barna Research Group, "Seven Paradoxes Regarding America's Faith," December 17, 2000.
7. Bruce Demarest, *Satisfy Your Soul* (Colorado Springs, CO: NavPress, 1999), p. 159.
8. E. M. Bounds, *The Complete Works of E. M. Bounds on Prayer* (Grand Rapids, MI: Baker Books, 1990), p. 371.

PART TWO

Start the Encounter

CHAPTER FIVE

The Priority of Pastoral Leadership

A few years ago I was in a midwestern city teaching a seminar on the priority of corporate prayer in the local church. A middle-aged woman approached me. After introducing herself, her eyes filled with tears as she struggled to communicate a heavy burden. Finally, she shared with intense emotion her deep love for her pastor, a great concern for his busy schedule and her sincere heartache over his lack of interest in the prayer ministry of the church. She knew that until he led the way, their congregation would continue to struggle to become a true house of prayer. Her concern was in knowing how to approach and encourage him without adding a burden of guilt or obligation.

The Indispensable Influencer

Over the years I've encountered many church members who desire a greater prayer emphasis in their congregation, yet the primary obstacle to this vision often can be the pastor. Many pastors feel inadequate to lead their congregations into deeper levels of prayer, while others are apathetic or overloaded with other things.

There is no way to overstate the vital role of the senior pastor in the church prayer ministry. The prayer life of the church will seldom rise above the pastor's personal example and commitment. Exodus 33:7-11 shows the prayerful example of Moses encountering God in the "tent of meeting" and motivating all the people to arise and worship. In Acts 6:1-7 the apostles' stalwart resolve to give themselves continually to "prayer and the ministry of the word" created an environment of increased supernatural impact.

> *The prayer life of the church will seldom rise above the pastor's personal example and commitment.*

In churches across the country today, congregations are eager for a greater emphasis on prayer. They want guidance and help in seeking God. They look to their pastor for consistent example and passionate leadership. But it is oftentimes not there when it comes to prayer.

A Pastor's Passion for Prayer

From my personal struggles and interactions with many of my peers, I discovered five basic reasons why pastors sometimes resist leading the way to a dynamic prayer ministry in the local church:

1. Many grew up in a prayerless church environment.

There is a Brazilian proverb that states, "The heart cannot taste what the eyes have not seen." Today's pastors often lack firsthand experience of what a dynamic prayer-energized church looks like.

Many pastors recall sparsely attended prayer meetings they've attended in the past. These sleepy prayer sessions featured a litany of personal requests or those for a third cousin twice removed. Accordingly, some pastors are happy if they can provide such a prayer gathering for three people who want to unload their various burdens. But a church where the majority of the people gather in dynamic, worship-based prayer does not register on most pastors' radar screens.

2. Most were trained in a prayerless educational process.

I went through seven years of formal undergraduate and graduate-level theological education at excellent institutions. While grateful for all the fine classes and grand truths, I never had a professor or pastor personally influence me in the area of prayer. Oh, there were great sermons on prayer and theological truths about prayer, but no one took me aside and taught me to pray by praying together on a regular basis.

Today, church leaders commonly receive many years of instruction about the ministry of the Word, while practical mentoring on the prayer ministry in the local church is neglected completely.

Few churches offer real teaching and practical instruction on prayer. The churches of my youth did not—or if they did, it certainly did not capture my attention. So how was I to learn? How do other pastors catch the passion?

3. All minister in a prayerless, success-oriented culture.

"Man of prayer" no longer ranks high on the typical list of desirable leadership traits for the local church pastor. Usually, the driven, over-achieving, "can-do" person is most admired in our society—and our churches.

> *"Man of prayer" no longer ranks high on the typical list of desirable leadership traits for the local church pastor.*

Recently, I was in Utah teaching a prayer seminar at a statewide church leadership conference. After my session, a man approached me explaining that he was the chairman of the pastoral search committee for a congregation in that area. He pulled out a list of more than eighty-five desirable attributes for their next pastor. The inventory had been compiled through a recent survey of the congregation. Many of the qualities centered on communication skills, management ability, pleasant personality, and strong pastoral care interests. Nowhere on the list was there any mention of the priority of prayer as an essential characteristic for the new pastor.

American society tends to value strong, natural leadership, dynamic programming, entertaining services, and impressive technology. The idea of a pastor locked away in extended prayer does not strike the average churchgoer as a mark of effective leadership. Some church members think it wastes time if the pastor spends energy attending prayer meetings. Many pastors realize this and decide not to go against the grain.

4. Some battle a prayerless personal life.

It is hard to take the church further than you have journeyed in your life. This sense of failure and guilt immobilizes many pastors in the church prayer ministry. Pastors know they should be leading the way, but as one leader wrote, "If I wished to humble anyone, I should question him about his prayers. I know nothing to compare with this topic for its sorrowful self confessions."[1] These unfortunate confessions often lead to unnecessary excuses. As a result the prayer ministry is without leadership and everyone suffers.

5. Every pastor is a special target of the enemy.

The "Master of Distraction" does not have to lure your pastor into scandalous sin. He simply needs to distract your pastor with good church activities. As long as the primary leader does not tap into the supernatural work of prayer, the church will be content to engage in a nice, socially pleasing ministry, but will have little Spirit-empowered impact.

For the Pastor

What if you are a pastor in need of a greater passion for prayer?
If you are a pastor, be assured my intention is not to dish out guilt but to encourage you with hope. Believe me, if God can chisel away at me to infuse a passion for prayer, He can do the same for you in an equally powerful (probably more powerful) fashion.

Reading this book is a great start. These pages come from a pastor's heart to a pastor's heart. This collection of teaching is full of my confessions of failure and stories of my hard-earned successes in prayer. I long that it will be a tool you can use over and over again.

Throughout the years, I have asked the Lord, as did the disciples, to teach me to pray. Ask for the desire to desire Him, for the thirst to thirst for Him, for the longing to long after Him. He wants you to be a man of prayer. Cooperate with His interests through eager and submissive prayers.

> *Learning to lead in prayer is not so much an issue of becoming informed, but a matter of getting infected.*

Pastor, expose yourself to other praying churches. Learning to lead in prayer is not so much an issue of becoming informed, but a matter of getting infected. Attend some conferences on prayer, especially those sponsored by and in a local-church laboratory. Some excellent ones are put together each year by Strategic Renewal International, the Church Prayer Leaders Network, and other prayer organizations. Or go to a Pastors' Prayer Summit. Go to www.prayersummits.net to find locations near you. Watch how other pastors lead prayer meetings. Prayer leadership is more caught than taught.

Finally, get started. Do not let the devil keep you in his clutches through guilt over your past failures or subjective feelings of inadequacy. My preferred style of leadership in prayer is borrowed from the Nike advertising theme "Just Do It." Start somewhere. Start today. Endure in faith. Your personal prayer life will deepen as you lead the way in corporate prayer.

You should recognize that the spiritual battle may heat up after you start praying. Satan is glad to ignore a prayerless preacher. When you start praying, you pose a new threat. But remember, you are a soldier in this life, not a sightseer. Battle is what we do if we are called to serve the King of kings. If we are not a "praying menace" to the enemy, we've missed our calling.

> *If we are not a "praying menace" to the enemy, we've missed our calling.*

Another excellent resource to check out is www.prayingpastor. com. This website and ministry, sponsored by the Church Prayer

Leaders Network, provides encouragement and resources to aid you as you seek to become a man or woman of prayer. It will provide help in developing your prayer leadership skills.

Some of the later chapters of this book will give you practical conviction, vision, and equipping for long-haul leadership. Read on.

For the Lay Person
What can you do if your pastor does not have a passion for prayer?
Rather than becoming discouraged or critical, church members can commit to five key initiatives:

1. Intercede on behalf of your pastor.
If you believe in the power of prayer, put it into action by asking God to move in your pastor's heart and life to make him a man of prayer. Pray in faith, knowing God wants His church to be a house of prayer and His leaders to be examples of this important priority. It is hard to be critical when you pray regularly for your pastor. Be patient and enduring as God works to make your leader a praying leader. Go to www.prayingpastor.com for help. While mainly for pastors, this website also provides materials on how to pray for your pastor.

2. Initiate a ministry of prayer in the church.
It is better to light a candle than to curse the darkness, so strike a positive flame of prayer. With the blessing and approval of your pastor, launch a strategic prayer ministry in the church. Begin with a focus that will bring special blessing to the church leadership.

> *It is better to light a candle than to curse
> the darkness so strike a positive flame of prayer.*

I recommend a time of intercessory prayer, preceding or concurrent with the Sunday morning church services. Even if you rotate participants, the pastor will appreciate powerful prayer support as he preaches. Of course, a leadership-oriented intercessory focus can be sponsored anytime during the week.

Join the Church Prayer Leaders Network. This ministry provides encouragement, resources, and challenge for people just like yourself—those who want to see prayer become more foundational in their church. Go to www.prayerleader.com for more information.

3. Invite your pastor (without guilt).

You cannot coerce the pastor into a burden for prayer ministry. However, a gracious invitation to "stop in sometime" would be fitting. As he sees the vibrancy, love, and support of praying saints, he will be moved by the potential of this focus and attracted to the excitement and possibility of prayer. Honey always works better than vinegar. Many a pastor has been turned off from a "prayer ministry" by guilt-oriented intercessors who meant well but manipulated too aggressively.

4. Inspire your pastor through practical resources.

Books, articles, audiocassettes, and videos, passed on by well-meaning parishioners, bombard most pastors. Be selective and thoughtful. But when you come across an article, audiocassette, or CD (These are easier to review than books or videos.), pass it on with grace and enthusiasm. Include a typed, executive summary to help your pastor understand why reading or listening will bless him.

Buy your pastor a subscription to *Pray!* magazine or pay for a membership for him in the Church Prayer Leaders Network (he will receive *Pray!* as a part of the benefits of membership). *Pray!* is the best tool I know to fuel a practical vision for prayer in the church. I serve on the editorial review board of this important publication and always appreciate the articles, especially those targeted to pastors.

Perhaps God will use this material to grab your pastor's attention and heart. Again, do not put a guilt trip on him about reading or listening. Pray he will.

5. Inform your pastor about prayer opportunities.

Periodically you can tap into prayer events that might inspire your pastor. It may be another church or a conference with a primary thrust on prayer. It is always best if another pastor leads this event and the focus is local-church oriented. (Pastors are leery of traveling "experts" who do not slug it out every day in the trenches of local church ministry.)

Get crazy and pay for a three-day trip to New York City for your pastor and his spouse. Ask them to attend the Tuesday evening prayer meeting at the Brooklyn Tabernacle, or if there is a praying church within close proximity, take a trip with your pastor to that area.

With some advance planning, you may be able to find a prayer conference that is local and church-focused. Give him adequate time to work it into his schedule and pay his way to attend. Consider sponsoring the spouse also. Include some other perks (a sports event, musical, or nice dinner) in case the "prayer thing" is not enough to get him there. Maybe a firsthand encounter with other pastors who have caught and implemented the prayer vision will be a key to sparking a personal vision for prayer in his church.

Encourage your pastor to call or email me if he is willing. You can get contact information at www.atgrace.com. I would be glad to host your pastor at my church and share all I can to "infect" him with a fresh vision and practice in prayer. Helping pastors is my greatest joy.

Working with the Lord to Make It Happen

Terry lives in a Northern California foothill town. He attended a three-day prayer retreat sponsored by Arcade Church in 1997. On his own, he could not seem to pray effectively and struggled with a critical attitude toward the leadership of his church. Through this extended time, praying in concert with scores of men, he learned how to pray for his church leaders with a loving and tender heart.

He returned several times to the Prayer Summits. On various occasions men gathered around Terry to pray for him. Through this experience he gained a fresh passion for biblical truth and a renewed understanding of genuine humility. He wrote these words in a recent letter of testimony: "I left these Prayer Summits with a renewed prayer vision for my church and life. I now recognize that what happened there God always intended for men of God to do on a continuous basis."

Today Terry supports his pastor with a genuine loyalty. God is using him to teach many other men in his church how to pray. His pastor has attended several Prayer Summits now and has been infected by the power of corporate prayer. Together they have launched weekly prayer meetings and sponsored an annual men's prayer retreat, patterned after the first one Terry attended at our church.

In God's providence, I ran into Terry two days before finishing this chapter. He was ecstatic. Fifty men from his 160-member church had just returned from their second annual prayer retreat. He could not contain himself as he related all God had done to renew and transform the participants. Terry's eyes filled with tears as he described the loving partnership he enjoyed with his pastor as they co-led this prayer event.

His pastor stood in the pulpit last Sunday and declared this retreat to be the most significant spiritual experience of his entire Christian life. It appears an awakening has begun in this foothill community—they had a fresh encounter. Terry has learned to pray. He caught a fresh vision for encouraging the spiritual leadership of his pastor and began to intercede to this end. His pastor has been infected and is now giving convincing and courageous leadership to the congregation.

Christ desires His church to be a house of prayer and wants pastors to lead the way. With this assurance you can lead the way as a pastor or proceed in faith to serve as a positive catalyst to fuel your pastor's vision for prayer.

Endnote

1. Dean C. J. Vaughan as quoted by Oswald Sanders, *Spiritual Leadership* (Chicago: Moody Press, 1994), p. 85.

CHAPTER SIX

Who Can Lead
an Encounter?

*P*astor Jim invited eight church members to join him at a prayer conference hosted by our church. As he hoped, the conference stirred their souls and imaginations. They wanted more from God than just another program. One of his members expressed this sentiment: "I'm challenged to learn more about what it means to seek God's face, not just His hand. All I want now, more than ever, is to experience God, not just know about Him."

Since the conference they are changing their church schedule to accommodate more prayer and stronger intimacy with God. The leaders are taking this calling seriously. The women in the church sensed God leading them in planning their next retreat to focus on worship-based prayer. Alice Moss, a gifted and godly leader whose heart has been touched to help facilitate the prayer movement, spoke at the retreat. God moved in some marvelous ways to heal hearts, restore marriages, and call women to new levels of ministry.

Pastor Jim, leading his church to pray, says, "I'm excited as more of our people catch the vision of worshiping at the feet of our magnificent Savior and becoming a true house of prayer."

This is how it happens. A pastor is stirred to take the lead. He begins to recruit and train others to help him direct the prayer movement. They are passionate and persevering. Fresh encounters with Christ begin.

> *Soon I realized that the prayer movement would never grow beyond my capacity to show up to everything.*

For many years I faltered in my effort to mobilize a dynamic prayer movement in the church. I failed to reproduce other leaders. Soon I realized that the prayer movement would never grow beyond my capacity to show up at everything. Once I began to identify and equip others to lead the prayer ministry, the impact escalated.

What kind of convictions should a pastor have if he is to lead the church to higher ground? What kind of people are we looking for to help advance a dynamic prayer ministry?

An Uncompromising Conviction about the Priority of Prayer

Prayer in its simplest definition is depending on God. When we do not pray, we are saying, "Lord, I think I can live the Christian life on my own." As I already noted, "Prayerlessness is my declaration of independence from God."

There are many biblical examples of this conviction in prayer. The most powerful is our Lord Jesus Christ. He spent forty days in prayer and fasting prior to the launching of His ministry. He habitually rose early to pray (Mk. 1:35) and slipped away to the remote and quiet places to seek the Father (Mk. 6:46; Lk. 5:16). Jesus prayed all night before a major decision (Lk. 6:12). He modeled prayer before His disciples, often praying with them (Lk. 9:18,28-29; 11:1; 22:39). The Garden of Gethsemane was His "go to" place to commune in prayer during good and bad times (Lk. 22:40).

I remind our prayer leaders that the passion and consistency of Jesus is our model for prayer. If Jesus needed to pray—both alone and with others—how much more do we need to pray in this way?

For the effective prayer leader, the prayer model of the early church also cultivates this conviction. The ministry of the disciples was birthed in prayer, nurtured in prayer, preserved by prayer and directed by extraordinary seasons of prayer (Acts 1:13-14, 24; 2:42; 3:1; 4:24-31; 6:4; 9:40; 10:9; 12:5,12; 13:1-3).

> *Prayer is not a preface or an addendum to the work of the ministry. It is the work of the ministry.*

Paul's life also inspires prayerful dependence. In Acts, we see him demonstrating a keen commitment to pray (Acts 14:23, 16:25, 20:36, 21:5). He regularly commented on the faithful prayers he offered on behalf of the churches and his need for their prayer in return. (Rom. 1:9, 15:30-33; Eph. 6:18-20; Philippians 1-4, Colossians 1-3, 4:2-4; 1 Thess. 3:10; 2 Thess. 1:11; 2 Tim. 1:3; Philemon 4). Prayer was his conviction. These models motivate us to be persons of prayer.

E. M. Bounds wrote:

> Prayer cannot be retired as a secondary force in this world. To do so is to retire God from the movement. It is to make God secondary. The prayer ministry is an all-engaging force. It must be so to be a force at all. The estimate and place of prayer is the estimate and place of God. To give prayer the secondary place is to make God secondary in life's affairs. To substitute other forces of prayer retires God and materializes the whole movement.[1]

Someone said, "Nothing of eternal significance ever happens apart from prayer." I often say that prayer is not a preface or an addendum to the work of the ministry. It is the work of the ministry. When I work, I work; when I pray, God works.

An Enduring Commitment to the Ministry of Corporate Prayer

Leaders in prayer ministry are fully convinced that Christ desires His church to pray together, and they are committed for the long haul. We need to view corporate prayer, not as a program, but a lifestyle; not a temporary fix, but a lifelong focus.

Hundreds of times I have watched pastors get fired up about prayer. Perhaps they read a book on revival, attended a conference or came under the conviction of the Holy Spirit. But without a deeply held conviction to endure, the inspiration fades quickly and everything is back to status quo—only worse.

Prayer ministry can be most difficult and discouraging. Sometimes you can plod along for years with little interest or results in the church. I remember a number of years ago after more than a decade of intense prayer leadership, crying out to the Lord, "How long do I have to keep this up?"

In a clear way, the Lord directed my heart to a penetrating question, challenging me to endurance: "Daniel, how long will you brush your teeth, take a shower, eat breakfast, and get dressed?" I understood. It was as if the Lord said, "Why would you question the longevity of this paramount commitment any more than these other basic lifelong routines?" That settled it for me. Since then, I resolved that prayer ministry is my way of life until my final day on earth.

Many would-be prayer leaders start well and sputter miserably. I tell pastors everywhere I go that they need to develop a vision to die on their knees.

Of course, many preachers have a vision of dying in the pulpit. There are stories of guys preaching away, then the next moment— thunk!. . . they are gone . . . "in a flame of glory!"

My dream, and I hope yours as well, is to lead God's people humbly into His presence until my dying day. Finish the course! Corporate prayer in the quest for an awakening is not a short-term program, but a lifestyle to be developed. An authentic prayer life—and the vision for a praying church—is a marathon, not a sprint.

An Enduring Captivation with God's Worthiness

In addition to a vision to endure for a lifetime, every effective prayer leader needs a pure and persevering motivation. We will talk about this extensively in chapters 8 and 9.

In my life I came to this in another one of those "aha moments" with the Lord. For almost fifteen years I consistently participated in early-morning prayer meetings on Mondays with the men of our church. As you might guess, this is the worst day of the week to be at a 6 a.m. prayer time. After leading an early Sunday prayer time, preaching three times in the morning and often being engaged in afternoon and evening church activities, I am whipped.

> *I tell pastors everywhere I go that they need to develop a vision to die on their knees.*

Early one Monday morning as the alarm went off and I arose at 5:15, I asked the Lord, "Why am I doing this?" In a still small voice, the Spirit prompted my heart with these words, "I am worthy to be sought."

This clear motivation must sink its roots deep into the fabric of everything we do. My motive cannot be focused on the many things that can vacillate. The size of the crowd at the prayer meeting, the emotional dynamic of the prayer time, the weather outside and my awareness of energy can change from week to week. Sometimes we sense a mighty rushing wind; other times it is early-morning halitosis.

But the truth of who He is never changes. Every week—rain or shine, burgeoning crowds or a pitiful handful, feeling good or feeling bad—He is worthy. Never forget this: The only enduring motive for prayer is that God is worthy to be sought.

A Firm Conclusion about the Supernatural Nature of the Church

The Scriptures are crystal clear on this point. The prophet Zechariah reminds us of the supernatural nature of God's plan for His people when he writes, "'Not by might nor by power, but by my Spirit,' says the LORD Almighty" (Zech. 4:6). King Hezekiah faced a formidable opponent but was drawn to God's supernatural power and offered this reminder to His people: "Be strong and courageous. Do not be afraid or discouraged because of the king of Assyria and the vast army with him, for there is a greater power with us than with him. With him is only the arm of flesh, but with us is the LORD our God to help us fight our battles" (2 Chron. 32:7-8).

The Psalms are replete with reminders of our need for a supernatural source if our efforts are to really matter. Psalm 20:7 states, "Some trust in chariots and some in horses, but we trust in the name of the LORD our God." Psalm 33:16-18 carries this same theme:

> No king is saved by the size of his army; no warrior escapes by his great strength. A horse is a vain hope for deliverance; despite all its great strength it cannot save. But the eyes of the LORD are on those who fear him, on those whose hope is in his unfailing love.

Again in Psalm 44:3 we are told that, "It was not by their sword that they won the land, nor did their arm bring them victory; it was your right hand, your arm, and the light of your face, for you loved them."

Prayer transcends our best effort to grow a church or build a ministry. The church is not a corporation but a community of people. It is not an organization but an organism. It is not an enterprise for Christ but an experience of Christ. It is supernatural and can only meet His standards through supernatural means. Because of that, prayer is indispensable.

Jesus said I will build my church and the gates of hell will not prevail against it (see Mt. 16:18). Then, He set about to do that thing through common men and women whose first recourse was prayer. Our first recourse should be prayer. And effective pastors and prayer leaders recognize that.

Effective prayer leaders do all they can to support the vision and leadership of the church. But at their core, they are only content with the supernatural realities of ministry that are birthed in prayer. They will often seem to be dissatisfied with programs, budgets, attendance figures, and increasing activities. Usually by their prayerful nature, they are not critical of these things. But their hearts would desire to see everything—plans, programs, activities—birthed in prayer. When that happens, God can move beyond our natural abilities to His supernatural ones.

In a praying church every program takes on a new tone. Why? Because like Acts 13:2-3, plans are birthed, not in human planning, but in His presence. Every advancement is immediately recognized as a fruit of God's provision through people moving ahead on their knees. I once heard Jim Cymbala say, "The church must be more than the sum of its parts." That is what motivates a true prayer leader.

An Abiding Concern for God's Glory in the Church

I like to define God's glory as the manifestation of Christ's presence among His people and the magnification of His person by His people. That is the passion of prayer ministry.

Paul writes, "Now to Him who is able to do exceeding abundantly beyond all that we ask or think, according to the power that works within us, to Him be the glory in the church and in Christ Jesus to all generations forever and ever. Amen" (Eph. 3:20-21, NASB). That is it. To Him be the glory in the church because we are praying, and He is doing the unimaginable.

> *I like to define God's glory as the manifestation of Christ's presence among His people and the magnification of His person by His people.*

This is seen in Acts 4:13 where the unbelieving Jewish leaders took a look at two unsophisticated, uneducated, and unimpressive men named Peter and John. They were unlikely fishermen, with an uncommon passion for Christ, having unimaginable impact on the world. All these leaders could assess is that "they had been with Jesus." That's the glory of God.

This manifest *shekinah* in the Old Testament was a cloud by day and a fire by night. This was the symbol of God's presence and supernatural provision in the midst of His people.

In Exodus 32-34 we read of God removing His presence because of Israel's idolatrous folly with the golden calf. In essence He said to Moses, "You go on to the Promised Land and I will protect you all the way, because I am a God of my word. But my manifest presence will not go with you" (see Ex. 33:1-3). Immediately the people knew they were dead in the water. They mourned and repented.

Moses, once again, engaged in his ordinary extraordinary prayer mode by entering the "tent of meeting" to seek God's face and intercede. He essentially said, "Lord, your manifest presence is the only thing that makes us different from any one else in the world. If your presence does not go with us, we are not moving an inch" (see Ex. 33:15-16).

Distinctly Different

Do you ever wonder what makes Christians distinctive in today's world? The fish emblems on our cars? The crosses around our necks? The political parties we endorse? The moral standards we espouse? Or is it the undeniable sense of the presence of Jesus Christ in our lives and in our midst in the church?

Second Corinthians 3 and 4 shows that what Moses had was nothing compared to the "glory" that lives in us by the indwelling Spirit. As we seek Him and live by His Spirit, we are being transformed from "glory to glory" (2 Cor. 3:18, NASB). It is Jesus' manifest presence in our lives that changes the world. That glory manifests the truth and affects people's consciences as we continue to "behold him face to face" in biblical prayer.

As people pray together in powerful worship-based prayer, something happens to them! Average believers become kingdom people. And this brings results—God works in their lives to shape and refine them to His image.

I already noted the amazing description of what ought to impress people in our churches. First Corinthians 14 describes it this way: "If an unbeliever or someone who does not understand comes in while everybody is prophesying, he will be convinced by all that he is a sinner and will be judged by all, and the secrets of his heart will be laid bare. So he will fall down and worship God, exclaiming 'God is really among you'" (vv. 24-25).

God among you is the aim and ambition of a praying church. We don't impress people with our clever preaching, entertaining dramas, excellent music, padded pews, outstanding programs, or even our friendly atmosphere. These are fine and good. But the praying church sees a powerful vision far beyond these temporal things: The glory of God. Nothing more. Nothing less. Nothing else.

I remember reading a story about the life of David Brainerd, a missionary in the 1700s to the American Indians. Even though he died of tuberculosis at 29, his impact was indeed supernatural. Often, because of coughing up blood in excruciating pain, he fell off his horse while riding to the next mission outpost.

But the praying church sees a powerful vision far beyond these temporal things: The glory of God. Nothing more. Nothing less. Nothing else.

Brainerd's first journey to the Forks of the Delaware to reach that ferocious tribe resulted in a miracle of God that preserved his life and revered him among the Indians as a "Prophet of God." Encamped at the outskirts of the Indian settlement, Brainerd planned to enter the Indian community the next morning to preach to them the gospel of Christ. Unknown to him, his every move was being watched by warriors who had been sent out to kill him. F. W. Boreham recorded the incident:

But when the braves drew closer to Brainerd's tent, they saw the paleface on his knees. And as he prayed, suddenly a rattlesnake slipped to his side, lifted up its ugly head to strike, flicked its forked tongue almost in his face, and then without any apparent reason, glided swiftly away into the brushwood. "The Great Spirit is with the paleface!" the Indians said; and thus they accorded him a prophet's welcome.[2]

Brainerd rose from his knees to lead this tribe to Christ.

Like Brainerd, the modern-day church leader knows it is not cleverness of methodology, not force of personality, nor the size of our organization, but the manifestation of God's glory in Jesus Christ through a praying church. That's the awakening that can change the world.

Who can lead their church into a fresh encounter with the living Christ? You can—if you keep in mind that you are not trying to put together a clever program, or a razzle-dazzle prayer meeting. You are simply leading people to seek God together. You are not seeking Him to do things for you; you are seeking Him simply because He is worthy to be sought.

Endnotes

1. E. M. Bounds, *The Complete Works of E. M. Bounds on Prayer* (Grand Rapids, MI: Baker Books, 1990), p. 370.
2. Fred Barlow, *Profiles in Evangelism* (Murfreesboro, TN: Sword of the Lord Publishers, 1976).

Chapter Seven

More Caught Than Taught

W hether we realize it or not, all of us form our attitudes and approaches to prayer through the influence of others we've observed. That is why we need to lead others by example. Most people are eager to learn to pray—they just don't know how.

Gary Link is a prominent attorney and judge in Sacramento. His gregarious, outspoken, and aggressive personality make him very good at what he does. In his professional arena, he is never at a loss for words.

After coming to Christ in the mid-nineties, Gary's outgoing style became a powerful weapon for the gospel. God has used him to lead hundreds of colleagues, clients, and acquaintances to Christ in the last ten years. Yet, in spite of his extroverted and verbal style, Gary felt incredibly inhibited in prayer meetings.

Still, Gary had an eager heart to learn. Over the years he has attended hundreds of prayer gatherings, observing the style, articulation, and passion of other prayer warriors. Admitting his intimidation, he kept listening and learning.

Today, Gary prays powerfully. At the end of every worship service he is available to pray with people in need, and does so with deep thoughtfulness and keen application. He leads a "Pastor's Prayer Partners" ministry with great confidence and passion. It has been a process for this outgoing leader to learn to pray. But he learned to do it by following the example of others.

As you embark on this prayer journey toward an awakening in your church, ask God to make you an influencer in prayer. Later we will talk about methodologies and practical ideas for effective leadership. Here I want to encourage you in the most important aspect of prayer leadership—example.

The Power of a Modeled Life

A grandmother invited some folks over for dinner one night. Before dinner she was not feeling well and verbalized her regret over the pressure of the dinner preparations. Later, after the company arrived and they sat down to eat, she asked six-year-old Susie, her grandchild, to ask the blessing.

"I don't know how to pray," Susie said.

"Well, Susie, pray like you heard me praying earlier today." Susie prayed, "Okay. Dear Lord, why in the world did I invite all these people over for dinner? In Jesus' name, amen." She had learned from example. We all have to pray and live in such a way that our example teaches others to pray honestly, authentically, and biblically.

I have pictures on my office wall of those who had a great impact on my life. Some are relatives; others are mentors or pastors with whom I am acquainted. Under each picture I noted the character qualities I admire in each. Their example means more to me than their net worth, talent, skill, or preaching. When it comes to prayer, your greatest impact is example.

> *Our messages tell people what to do.*
> *Our lives show them how to do it.*

Our messages tell people what to do. Our lives show them how to do it. We tend to be long on sermons about prayer and short on modeling in prayer. The best way to help people pray is to pray with them. The praying church will look for ways to put people in contact with strong pray-ers. And they need to see authentic openness and vulnerability in prayer modelers.

Our three-day Prayer Summits give me the opportunity to lead people in a spontaneous form of prayer. With Bibles opened, we follow the Holy Spirit's direction, worshiping the Lord and reading hundreds of portions from God's Word. We seek to learn together to respond honestly and authentically to the truth.

Eventually, the intense worship and Scripture reading leads to a response in small gender-specific groups. In obedience to James 5:16, participants begin to confess their faults and weaknesses to one another in order to be prayed for. God uses this to create some powerful moments of forgiveness, restoration, and healing.

Without fail, the Lord grips my heart and I also share with the small group of men some of the struggles I encounter. In the traditional school of thought, pastors are not supposed to have cracks in their armor. Certainly, they should never talk about them. But I have learned that our men love and respect me more deeply because of my transparency. I also find that my example empowers them to be authentic with the Lord and real with one another.

The Contagious Influence of a Model

As I've noted earlier, the greatest hindrance to a movement of prayer in the church is often the absence of an exemplary leader. Exodus 33 (one of my favorites as you can tell) gives an excellent example of an Old Testament praying leader—Moses.

> Now Moses used to take a tent and pitch it outside the camp some distance away, calling it the "tent of meeting." Anyone inquiring of the LORD would go to the tent of meeting outside the camp. . . . As Moses went into the tent, the pillar of cloud would come down and stay at the entrance, while the LORD spoke with Moses. Whenever the people saw the pillar of cloud standing at the entrance to the tent, they all stood and worshiped, each at the entrance to his tent. The LORD would speak to Moses face to face, as

a man speaks with his friend. Then Moses would return to the camp, but his young aide *Joshua son of Nun did not leave the tent.* (Ex. 33:7-11, emphasis added).

These verses describe Moses' habits of meeting with the Lord. Moses responded at this moment of crisis in the same manner he lived every day as a matter of conviction. He set the pace by going out to the tent of meeting. As Moses spoke to God in face-to-face intimacy, the congregation of Israel was motivated to worship in their own lives.

People forget our sermons but will forever be marked by our example. At the end of the day, it is not what we said about prayer (or any other subject) as much as how we lived.

The example people observe in shared prayer moments is indispensable in mobilizing a new generation of prayer leaders. Don't slip past what this passage says about Joshua's encounter with God's presence, alongside Moses: "his young aide Joshua son of Nun did not leave the tent." That is powerful.

> *Moses responded at this moment of crisis in the same manner he lived every day as a matter of conviction.*

Moses took Joshua into the tent with him. This reminds us that the greatest way to teach people to pray is to ask them to come alongside us. It is no surprise that Joshua became the next leader for the children of Israel. The Lord was with him, just as He was with Moses. Only eternity will reveal the influence of the tent of meeting.

The experience of shared and extended seasons of prayer is a sorely neglected component of real discipleship. Discipleship simply is not sitting at Denny's enjoying a "Grand Slam" breakfast, filling in the blanks of a booklet. Real discipleship needs to include modeling prayer. Otherwise it is shortsighted.

The Compelling Instruction of Example

I am convinced that Jesus influenced the disciples more by His model in prayer than through His messages of prayer. We see a hint of this in Luke 11:1: "One day Jesus was praying in a certain place. When he finished, one of his disciples said to him, 'Lord, teach us to pray, just as John taught his disciples.'"

The disciples were with Jesus as He was praying. His example led to their hunger to learn. Watching Him pray gave them a thirst to do it themselves.

> *The best advice I can give to a person interested in a movement of prayer is make the first move. Just do it.*

The "Mount of Transfiguration" experience emerged from a prayer time with Jesus, Peter, James, and John. Jesus also called His disciples together to pray in the garden in the last week of His life.

The best advice I can give to a person interested in a movement of prayer is make the first move. Just do it. Let your model be the motivation for others.

The Compounding Impact of Example

In Acts 6, the apostles stood firm in the midst of an administrative crisis. They were overseeing a church of multiplied thousands. Their values stand in direct contrast to our society where prayer tends to take a back seat when we get busy and big.

Controversy was brewing over the breakdown of the food distribution program for the widows. The Bible is clear on the importance of caring for the widows (1 Tim. 5:3; Jas. 1:27).

Obviously, they were willing to fix this managerial problem by working, but would not have been wise to do so. They went for example rather than executive intervention. They delegated the job and stayed on task, setting the pace on their knees and in God's Word.

> "It would not be right for us to neglect the ministry of the word of God in order to wait on tables. Brothers, choose seven men from among you who are known to be full of the Spirit and of wisdom. We will turn this responsibility over to them and *[WE] will give our attention to prayer and*

the ministry of the word." This proposal pleased the whole group. . . . They presented these men to the apostles, who prayed and laid their hands on them. So the word of God spread. The number of disciples in Jerusalem increased rapidly, and a large number of priests became obedient to the faith. (Acts 6:2-7, emphasis added)

This is an inspiring reminder that when leaders lead by example, keeping dialed-in to the power source, the church moves into incredible realms of spiritual impact.

I'll never forget something I heard on a tape from Charles Tremendous-Jones, retired insurance executive and motivational speaker. I was so impacted by it that I replayed and reviewed the tape until I memorized it. I have long since lost the tape but will never forget the quote: "All the truth in the world will do you little good until God brings a person across your path and you are able to see that truth in action. Suddenly that truth becomes a driving force in your life."

That is why "the Word became flesh and made his dwelling among us. We have seen his glory, the glory of the One and Only, who came from the Father, full of grace and truth" (Jn. 1:14). Truth does transform. When truth is modeled it becomes a driving force in someone's life. People in churches all across our country are excited to learn to pray by following the example of leaders who will show them how, on their knees.

When you experience the truth of the power of corporate prayer, you need to share it as well. That is why churches that have dynamic, worship-based, corporate prayer meetings have no trouble growing them—and seeing their other prayer ministries grow as well. People who catch the vision, share it with others—and lives are changed.

PART THREE

Fueling the Encounter

CHAPTER EIGHT

The Right Thing
for the Wrong Reason

*J*ames Hastings, editor of *The Speaker's Bible*, tells about meeting a family facing starvation that came to him for help. Mr. Hastings, though comparatively well off, carried only half a crown in his pocket—enough for supper that night and breakfast the next day, but nothing for dinner the following day.

He told himself that if he had another coin, he would share it freely with the impoverished family. To quiet the battle within his conscience, he decided to pray for the family. As he knelt with them and began to pray, his conscience jabbed him. "Dare you mock God? Dare you kneel down and call Him Father with that half-crown in your pocket?" When he finished praying, he found no relief from the distress his conscience caused until he gave the man his coin.[1]

His story demonstrates how easy it is to pray with the wrong motive. In his case it was to soothe his conscience and avoid obedience. Like Hastings, we can do the right thing for the wrong reason, even in prayer.

In Matthew 6 Jesus exposed our battle with the motive issue as He pointed out the Pharisees whose holiness was full of holes because they were praying to be seen by men, rather than God.

> *I have learned that I can often do all the
> right things, but for all the wrong reasons.*

My journey in prayer has certainly been a painful discovery of higher and holier motives. I have learned that I can often do all the right things, but for all the wrong reasons. On the surface, I may appear very spiritual and dedicated. In my heart, I am still consumed with selfish interests and missing the reward He promises to the sincere seeker. We can pray for the wrong reasons and with the wrong motives, too.

I experienced and observed some typical, but misguided motives for participating in prayer gatherings.

Guilt

Because we know prayer is commanded, important, and expected, we feel obligated to attend prayer meetings and feel guilt if we don't. After all, the pastor announces it every week and encourages our participation. Yet guilt seldom sustains us in the cause and usually keeps us from enjoying the experience. In fact, when motivated by guilt, we look for the slightest excuse to not go to prayer meetings.

Acceptance

Many of us grew up in a performance-based environment where we were worthy of love only when we did things that were impressive and good. Systems of faith carried this over into the church life through a works-based acceptance with God. Many people think the more they pray the more God will love them. Some even believe that the pastor and other leaders will love them more if they go to prayer meetings. So they "perform" by attending.

We cannot make God love us any more or cause Him to love us any less. God loves us, not because of who we are or what we do. He loves us because of who He is. He cannot help it. God is love. We ought not to pray to be accepted by God. That was settled already at Calvary's cross.

> *God loves us, not because of who we are or what*
> *we do. He loves us because of who He is.*
> *He cannot help it because He is love.*

Church Growth

It is common in a world where "bigger is always better" to adopt prayer as the next and newest strategy for church growth. The logic goes, "If I pray, God will be pleased. If God is pleased, He will bless me. If He blesses me, my church will grow."

What we seldom admit is the potential that when our church grows, our ego will be gratified and our ecclesiastical status will soar. I learned through much soul-searching that while God delights in a praying people and is eager for the advancement of His church, He would not reduce something as pure and distinctive as prayer to the next strategy for our human-centered success.

I distinctly remember the day I sat in a session listening to Pastor Peter Lord speak about the priority of seeking God. He asked the pastors this question: "If God promised you two things: First, that you would go to Heaven when you die and second, that He would never use you again in the ministry; would you still pray?" It was like an arrow to my heart. In my passion to be used by God, I was using God for my egocentric purposes.

> *When prayer does not succeed as a church growth tool,*
> *it is discarded for a more "effective" methodology.*

This explains why prayer tends to come and go in some churches. When prayer does not succeed as a church growth tool, it is discarded for a more "effective" methodology.

Revival

In my progression toward a purer motive I embraced the vision for revival. What a noble ambition. Admittedly, I devoured everything written by Leonard Ravenhill and other revival writers.

In His gracious wisdom the Lord confronted me one day with a question as I listened to a speaker at a conference on revival (of which I was in charge!). He asked, "Are you seeking *revival from God* or are you seeking *God for revival?*"

Almost every Christian leader longs for revival. Of course, we secretly hope it starts in our denomination or church (not in that weird group of churches from another part of the country). Even this exposes how self-serving our interest in revival can be. We want an experience instead of God Himself.

I often wondered if, after the great revival came then subsided, *Would I still pray with the same passion?* I hope so.

God is birthing in my heart a desire for a revival that is so glorious, no one even cares how it started or who helped lead the way.

While a desire for revival seems a worthy motive to pray, the only enduring motive for prayer is that God is worthy to be sought. The church may or may not grow; revival may or may not come, but HE IS STILL WORTHY!

Endnote

1. R. Kent Hughes, *1001 Great Stories*, "Quotes" (Wheaton, IL: Tyndale House Publishers, 1998), pp. 318-322.

CHAPTER NINE

Seek His Face,
Not His Hand

A few years ago, a prayer craze seemed to explode upon us based on the phenomenal sales of a little book based on an obscure prayer. *The Prayer of Jabez,* by Bruce Wilkinson sold multi-millions of copies. In it Wilkinson shared the direction God gave him in ministry when he began praying the principles of that prayer. He challenged his readers that if we prayed that too, God would bless us—spiritually and through expanded ministry for Him—making a difference in the kingdom.

After the book had been out for a while controversy began to brew around it. It seems that many people thought they would get financial and material blessing if they prayed this prayer. They began praying selfishly, missing God's intention entirely. Many people were concerned with what God would do for them, instead of what they could do—with God's blessing—for Him.

There is a profound difference between request-based prayers and worship-based prayers. I've watched as this distinction transformed the way thousands of people pray, privately and in group gatherings. Broken down, it really is the difference between seeking God's hand and His face.

Of course, God is Spirit (Jn. 4:24) so the idea of His "hand" and "face" are concepts designed to help us understand how He works and how we should relate to Him. In general, His hand refers to what He does for me. His face is who He is to me.

If you develop a ministry of united prayer in your church through worship-based prayer, you and your people will experience God's hand in incredible ways. But His face will keep you praying. The beauty of who He is, the wonder of His character and the power of His name will become your primary passions. Why? Because God longs to be sought.

I enjoyed the story of a big company boss who called to check on his company's computer programmer who called in stating that he could not come to work because of a family crisis. The boss called the employee's house to check on him. A little boy whispered, "Hello?"

Feeling a bit put out because of the inconvenience of talking to a youngster, the boss said, "Young man, is your daddy home?"

"Yes."

"May I talk to him?"

To the surprise of the boss, the little boy said, "No."

Wanting to talk with an adult, the boss said, "Well, is your mommy home?"

"Yes."

"May I talk with her?"

"No."

Knowing it was unlikely a young child would be left home alone, he decided to leave a message with the person who might be watching the child. "Is there anyone besides you?"

"Yes, a policeman."

Wondering what a cop was doing in his employee's home, the boss asked, "May I speak with the policeman?"

"No, he's busy."

"Busy doing what?"

"Talking to daddy and mommy . . . and the fireman."

With growing concern the boss was not sure what to do. He heard what sounded like a helicopter in the background and said, "What's that noise?"

"It's a hello-copter."

The boss asked, "What's going on there?"

The boy whispered oddly, "The search team just landed the hello-copter." Alarmed and more than frustrated the boss asked, "Why are they there?"

The boy muffled his giggle. "They're looking for me."

I suspect the boss never got to talk to his computer programmer but he did observe a valuable lesson in human behavior through the example of the little boy. People love to be sought as the center of attention, even if it causes a ruckus.

One of the great devotional writers noted, "The main thing God asks for is our attention."[1] In a completely pure and holy way, God loves to be sought. He is glorified when we give our utmost effort to the discovery of His holy presence and person.

My favorite passage on this subject underscores the importance of this focus. "One thing I ask of the LORD, this is what I seek: that I may dwell in the house of the LORD all the days of my life, to gaze upon the beauty of the LORD, and to seek him in his temple. . . . My heart says of you, 'Seek his face!' Your face, LORD, I will seek" (Ps. 27:4,8).

Here God takes the initiative in calling us to seek Him. It is not the result of our astute spiritual instincts. Rather He initiates the interchange of intimacy. My heart responds to the invitation as I seek His face. It becomes the "one thing" of my life, especially my prayer life.

Exodus 33:11 presents a captivating commentary on what made Moses such a compelling example of prayer. "The LORD would speak to Moses face to face, as a man speaks with his friend." This is not the picture of a needy saint dutifully reviewing a list of requests. This shows a hungry God-seeker enjoying intimacy with the Almighty.

Later in this same encounter Moses prays: "If you are pleased with me, teach me your ways so I may know you and continue to find favor with you" (Ex. 33:13). While Moses needs to know God's plan, he ultimately desires God's person. That's where the blessing lies!

One of the more obscure but powerful challenges to prayer comes from Romans. Paul writes, "I urge you, brothers, by our Lord Jesus Christ and by the love of the Spirit, to join me in my struggle by praying to God for me" (Rom. 15:30).

> *When we limit ourselves to seeking*
> *His hand, we may miss His face.*

Paul calls for the church to gather in passionate, agonizing prayer. But, left to ourselves, we don't pray like that. It requires the supernatural "love of the Spirit." He also urges us to pray, "By our Lord Jesus Christ" (literally, out of regard for Christ). Here again we see that our prayer for His hand to work starts with His face in view.

Remember, the only enduring motive for prayer is that God is worthy to be sought. Since His worthiness will be the central focus of our worship in eternity, we are wise to make it the impetus to our prayers on earth. "You are worthy our Lord and God, to receive glory and honor and power, for you created all things, and by your will they were created and have their being" (Rev. 4:11).

I learned over the years that when we limit ourselves to seeking His hand, we may miss His face. He will provide because He is a loving and caring Father, but we may miss the intimacy He intends for us. Conversely, when we seek His face, He delights in opening His hand.

When a Church Seeks His Face

Multiplied thousands around the world have experienced this principle. Our three-day Prayer Summits are based entirely on the foundation of seeking Him. Everything centers in spontaneous Scripture reading and worship in song and praise.

I often say that worship is the response of all I am to the revelation of all He is. We focus on revelation—intense, pure, free-flowing worship from the Word. Out of this pursuit, an incredible response naturally occurs as God opens His hand to convict, restore, and transform.

One elder in the church went to his first Prayer Summit with great trepidation. He asked himself, "What am I going to talk to God about for three days?" After his first Summit he admitted, "I was asking the wrong question. The right question was: What was God going to talk to me about for three days?" This is a beautiful snapshot of the transition from a life of "talking to God" through request-based prayer to worship-based prayer, letting God speak to the heart in worship.

Worship is the response of all I am to the revelation of all He is.

A Forty-Day Spiritual Discovery

Starting in 1999, our church initiated an annual Forty-Day Spiritual Discovery. Each year we write forty days of personal Bible studies for adults, youth, and children. These devotional guides correlate directly with the preaching themes. We encourage everyone to consider some form of fasting. Some engage in a food fast while others abstain from desserts, television, shopping, secular music, or chocolate. One man told me he was going to fast from tithing. Fortunately, he was joking.

We sponsor additional prayer opportunities during this intense season of united spiritual pursuit. Many individual breakthroughs occur as people accelerate their holy habits. Corporately, the primary focus is to seek God and His agenda for our church.

For many years prior, I led the church in a "vision" process that usually amounted to an imitation of what some other church was trying. We would read books, go to conferences and meet around a conference table, brainstorming our vision with dry-erase pens on a white board.

God showed us that real vision comes when we seek Him, not a vision. In Acts 13:1-3 the early church leaders were "worshiping the Lord and fasting." There is no indication they were seeking God for what to do with Saul and Barnabas. They were just in God's presence, in willing, waiting worship. While worshiping, vision and direction came. They did not arrive at vision through imitation but through inspiration.

Following that pattern, we have learned that God entrusts His most fruitful plans to those who maintain the most focused passion. For example, one particular year our church leaders felt compelled to pursue a fresh vision for ministry at the conclusion of our "discovery." These new initiatives would involve a twenty-five percent increase in giving to the general ministry fund.

There was not a giving trend to support this kind of increase. Our management team appealed to the elders to reconsider this radical increase. Yet, as a result of our united time of fasting and prayer, we felt convinced about the importance of this step of faith.

Every week we brought this need before the church at the Thursday night Fresh Encounter. No giving campaigns were launched. No sermons on financial stewardship were preached. We simply prayed. When the new fiscal year arrived, the church overwhelmingly voted to affirm the dramatically increased budget.

Without any human explanation, we discovered that two months into the new budget year the giving was seven percent ahead of the twenty-five percent increase. In spite of the 9/11 crisis later that year the giving still met the increased budget. The elders and congregation were astounded to observe the power of what can happen when a church really prays.

Year after year His Spirit has transformed our hearts and the very culture of our church. He has provided miraculously for His work and blessed our ministry, simply because we learned to seek His face, not just His hand.

I have learned that God is always willing to oblige when we give Him our undivided attention. When we seek His face, He draws us close in intimacy then opens His hand with pleasure.

What Do We Really Want?

If I had a conversation with you and you happened to be holding a $100 bill, I could approach you in two ways. I could act as if I had an interest in you, but spend the entire moment fixed with my eyes and attention on the money in your hand. You would feel that the conversation was cheapened by my greed and my interest in you may seem ungenuine.

On the other hand, I could look you straight in the eye, showing a genuine interest in you and the relationship, unfazed by your $100 bill. In this case, you might be inclined to invite me to dinner, using the money to buy us a meal.

It is a simple illustration but so apropos to our approach in prayer. Seek Him, not just His gifts. He is a good God, ready to bless you. But ultimately He made you for Him, not you.

> *God entrusts His most fruitful plans to those who maintain the most focused passion.*

I spoke about Bob and Joyce Bridges in chapter 2. In a recent conversation, Bob told of how his PSA (cancer count) has escalated to over 180, a dangerously high diagnosis. Unfazed, and full of joy, Bob reminded me of the passage God used to transform the focus of his life. Psalm 105:3-4 reads, "Glory in his holy name; let the hearts of those who seek the LORD rejoice. Look to the LORD and his strength; *Seek his face* always" (emphasis added).

Bob has learned the importance and the impact of seeking God's face. A. B. Simpson, pastor and founder of The Christian and Missionary Alliance, communicated his grasp of this passion with these poignant words in his poem "Himself":

Once it was the blessing,
Now it is the Lord;
Once it was the feeling,
Now it is His Word.
Once His gifts I wanted,
Now the Giver own;
Once I sought for healing,
Now Himself alone.

Once 'twas painful trying,
Now 'tis perfect trust;
Once a half salvation,
Now the uttermost.

Once 'twas ceaseless holding,
Now He holds me fast;
Once 'twas constant drifting,
Now my anchor's cast.

Once 'twas busy planning,
Now 'tis trustful prayer;
Once 'twas anxious caring,
Now He has the care.
Once 'twas what I wanted
Now what Jesus says;
Once 'twas constant asking,
Now 'tis ceaseless praise.

Once it was my working,
His it hence shall be;
Once I tried to use Him,
Now He uses me.
Once the power I wanted,
Now the Mighty One;
Once for self I labored,
Now for Him alone.

Once I hoped in Jesus,
Now I know He's mine;
Once my lamps were dying,
Now they brightly shine.
Once for death I waited,
Now His coming hail;
And my hopes are anchored
Safe within the veil.[2]

Endnotes

1. As quoted by Jim Cymbala, *Fresh Wind Fresh Fire* (Grand Rapids, MI: Zondervan, 1997) p. 57.
2. A. B. Simpson., "Himself," (Camp Hill, PA: Christian Publications, Inc., 1885, 1990). From the booklet *Himself.*

PART FOUR

Vision for an Encountering Community

CHAPTER TEN

Experience the Encounter Together

*B*illy, motivated and endowed with athletic skills, dreamed of becoming a star baseball player. Unfortunately, his little league coach was not familiar with the keys to a winning game. Rather than gathering his eager players for regular practice, Billy's coach sent the players home every day with a ball, bat, and glove to practice the game—alone. Billy tried to reach proficiency in baseball, but struggled with a deep sense of frustration about the game.

Each weekend Billy's group lined up against an opposing squad, but could not win a game. They never learned to play together as a team. By the end of the season Billy's dream of the big leagues faded.

If his coach had understood that baseball is a team sport, he could have propelled Billy's ambitions to reality. If the coach valued team practice, Billy and his teammates could have tasted the thrill of victory. Instead, the coach's lack of awareness squandered Billy's potential and caused youthful ambitions to vanish.

Many pastors believe prayer is more an individual sport, not a team sport. They send eager church members home each week to practice in solitude. Frustrated by their inability to excel, many give up their hopes of praying with consistency and conviction. Dreams die. Individuals give up. The team never excels.

> *Many pastors believe prayer is more an individual sport, not a team sport.*

Some things are meant to be shared. In the normal course of daily life we share our birthday parties, anniversaries, weddings, meals and sports leagues with friends and family. In our faith there are certain activities that we best experience in community—worship, communion, fellowship, baptisms and, yes, prayer.

A Culture of Individuals

In our Western culture we seem to believe it is more important to pray alone than with others. This is a symptom of our basic view of society. In his book, *The Connecting Church,* Randy Frazee describes ours as a culture of "individualism." He notes that we no longer are born into a culture of community but a "way of life that makes the individual supreme or sovereign over everything."[1]

Frazee documents this as a problem, especially for those born after World War II. He laments the impact on the church in that we have "all too often mirrored the culture by making Christianity an individual sport."[2]

Alexis de Tocqueville noted that prior societies did not even have a word for individualism.[3] They had no conception of an individual who did not belong to a group and who could be considered absolutely alone. One observer said that we have become a society of *solo sapiens.*[4]

As it relates to prayer, we have lost the New Testament conviction that we must pray together, first, if we are to learn to pray alone.

"Why have we neglected the corporate emphasis on prayer found in Acts and the epistles?" Gene Getz asks that question in his book, *Praying for One Another,* and tells how we view biblical prayer from our bias rather than from the original intent and context of the Scriptures. He agrees that our Western culture stresses rugged individualism:

> We use the personal pronouns "I" and "my" and "me." We have not been taught to think in terms of "we" and "our" and "us." Consequently, we individualize many references to corporate experience in the New Testament, thus often emphasizing personal prayer. More is said in Acts and the Epistles about corporate prayer, corporate learning of biblical truth, corporate evangelism, and corporate Christian maturity and growth than about the personal aspects of these Christian disciplines.
>
> Don't misunderstand. Both are intricately related. But the personal dimensions of Christianity are difficult to maintain and practice consistently unless they grow out of a proper corporate experience on a regular basis.[5]

A prayer leader needs conviction that the Bible commands us to pray together. This conviction springs from a fresh awareness of scriptural teaching on prayer and gives a prayer leader endurance in his or her ministry.

> *The personal dimensions of Christianity are difficult to maintain and practice consistently unless they grow out of a proper corporate experience on a regular basis.*

The Early Church Community

It is clear that Jesus took it for granted that the church would experience prayer in body-life. We see many applications of this community approach to prayer. We will look specifically at His landmark teaching from "The Lord's Prayer" in Matthew 6, in the next chapter.

After His ascension Jesus told His small band of followers to wait for the promise of the Holy Spirit. Rather than separating into their private "prayer closets" at home, they stayed together for ten days in the upper room. Acts 1:14 gives a record of their focus: "They all joined together constantly in prayer, along with the women and Mary the mother of Jesus, and with his brothers."

In contrast to our modern-day mindset, early Christians possessed a community spirit. "What we do, we do together." That idea became real to them. How foreign it is to our American culture.

Because of their strong understanding of genuine community, the early church regularly prayed together. Corporate prayer was central to launching the church (Acts 1:14, 2:1). New believers at once immersed themselves in prayer with other believers as essential to their spiritual nurture (Acts 2:42). The church coped with crisis and persecution together on their knees (Acts 4:24-31). As the church grew, the apostles refused to become embroiled in administrative problems because they resolved to model prayer in their leadership team (Acts 6:4). Through united prayer they trusted God for miraculous, divine interventions in times of extreme trouble (Acts 12:5-12). They received ministry direction through intense seasons of worshipful prayer (Acts 13:1-2).

How different from our individualized culture. We were taught prayer is something *I* do on *my* own in a closet somewhere. We will examine the idea of the "closet" in the next chapter.

Our Assumptions about Prayer

Today we read the commands about prayer in the New Testament epistles and take for granted that they are designed primarily to motivate the individual believer during his private prayer time. We now believe that prayer is first and best experienced at a private level. We assume that only a select few will enjoy praying in concert with others. I suggest the early Christians held a very different perspective.

Author Michael Griffiths provides essential insight when he writes:

Many of the commonest expressions used in the New Testament to describe the church are plural nouns such as brethren, children, saints, disciples, or collective nouns such as flock, nation and people.

To illustrate this he notes:

This tendency is reflected in the way in which we sing about our faith. This can be demonstrated very simply by picking up any of the popular hymn books in everyday use and noting how very many "I" and "my" hymns there are, and how relatively few "we" and "our" hymns there are, which are really suitable congregational singing. Most of our hymns would be much more suitable as solos! It is as though most Christians expect to fly solo to heaven with only just a little bit of formation flying from time to time.

Griffiths then points out:

the plural form "saints" occurs some sixty-one times. Only once (Phil. 4:21) is the singular used. . . . The concept of a solitary saint is foreign to the New Testament writers. The idea of the hermit of solitary religious recluse, far from being biblical in origin, seems to be more the product of an escapist type of extreme separatism.[6]

It is good to remember that until the advent of the printing press, God's Word was experienced primarily in community as Christians heard the truth explained within their regular gatherings. Obviously, there were doctrinal abuses during those centuries, but the basic approach to learning was auditory and corporate.

Today, most Christians enjoy a personal copy of the Bible. Fortunately, this increases our knowledge and learning of Scripture through private study and personal devotions. Unfortunately, it fuels our hyper-individualistic approach to the Christian life, including prayer.

> *Our culture and mindset affect our approach to interpreting Scripture. When we read about the need to pray, we usually assume this primarily applies to private prayer experience.*

Our culture and mindset affect our approach to interpreting Scripture. When we read about the need to pray, we usually assume this primarily applies to private prayer experience.

Michael Griffiths repeats this consideration when he writes,

> In standard English, the second person singular "you" and the second person plural "you" are identical. Thus, New Testament Letters addressed to congregations are read (by us) as though they were addressed to the individuals. It is good and right that we should apply the Scriptures to ourselves personally, but it is unfortunate if we also apply the Scriptures individualistically and ignore the fact that the original intention was to instruct us not so much as individuals, but as whole communities of Christian people.[7]

We fail to comprehend that the early churches experienced the truth of God's Word in community, not individually. Consider a first century arrival of a letter from the apostle Paul. The believers gathered eagerly and listened with united hearts and ears to hear what they should do together to better please Christ. What we presume should be done alone, they instinctively first practiced together, then did it on their own.

Seeing Prayer through the Eyes of the Early Church

Let's reexamine some common commands about prayer, which we normally take for granted. Consider what the early believers probably understood. Look at these passages through new lenses— lenses of the early church culture.

Prayer Passage	Individualistic Interpretative Lens of Modern Christianity	Community Interpretative Lens of the Early Church
"I urge you, brothers, by our Lord Jesus Christ and by the love of the Spirit, to join me in my struggle by praying to God for me." (Ro. 15:30)	With the help of Christ and the Holy Spirit in my life, I need to pray hard for leaders who spread God's Word.	Because of Christ, we need to continually gather to pray for Paul with an agonizing passion that comes from the love of the Holy Spirit.
". . . he will continue to deliver us, as you help us by your prayers. Then many will give thanks on our behalf for the gracious favor granted us in answer to the prayers of many." (2 Cor. 1:10b-11)	I need to pray for those who preach the Word. I should be thankful when God answers my prayers.	When we gather to pray for those who lead and preach, we can rejoice together when we see our prayers answered.
"And pray in the Spirit on all occasions with all kinds of prayers and requests. With this in mind, be alert and always keep on praying for all the saints." (Eph. 6:18)	I need to learn to pray in many ways for many people as the Spirit fills my heart and helps me persevere in prayer.	We need to gather and persevere in all kinds of prayer for all kinds of people as we are led by the Holy Spirit.
"Devote yourselves to prayer, being watchful and thankful." (Col. 4:2)	I need to dedicate myself to prayer with an alert mind and grateful heart.	We need to continually devote ourselves to pray together with alertness and gratitude.
"Pray without ceasing." (1 Thess. 5:17, NASB)	I need to maintain an attitude of prayerfulness throughout my day.	We need to gather together in constant prayer in the church.
"Finally, brothers, pray for us that the message of the Lord may spread rapidly and be honored, just as it was with you." (2 Thess. 3:1)	Because God's Word has blessed my life, I need to pray for the success of those who preach it to others.	We saw the power of God's Word in our midst and need to pray together for this same impact in other churches as it is preached.

The Impact of Learning to Pray with Others

I believe church leaders make a huge mistake when they assume that Christians are learning to pray individually. By simply talking about prayer and sending them home to learn alone we have multiplied frustration, bred failure, and ignored the basic tenets of New Testament community. One of the biggest reasons churches suffer from a lack of prayer is that we assume our people are praying. Most are not!

If we are satisfied with the current level of prayer in our church, we do not need to change a thing. If not, we must change the way we think about prayer, interpret the prayer commands, and teach people to pray. The positive results will be dramatic.

Pastor Alan, a pastor of Chinese descent, leads a church with three congregations. One is English-speaking while the other two worship in the Chinese dialects of Mandarin and Cantonese. Over the years, he became very discouraged with dull, sparsely attended, request-based prayer meetings. Eventually, he gave up the vision, cancelled the corporate prayer times and simply encouraged people to pray on their own at home.

A few years ago, Alan's wife attended a three-day Prayer Summit sponsored by our church. She returned home with great enthusiasm and ignited a fresh vision for corporate prayer among the women. A few months later, Pastor Alan, his wife, and several key leaders from his church attended a prayer conference sponsored by our church. With fresh inspiration and equipping, he re-established a worship-based weekly prayer time in the church. Soon he attended one of our seminars, featuring the principles of this book. His vision and conviction grew.

As I finish this chapter I am looking at a recent email I received from Pastor Alan. It came on the heels of our most recent prayer conference. This dear pastor expressed words of deep appreciation for his profound rediscovery of the power of corporate prayer. He and his wife had thirty-three people from their church at the conference. They all were infected with fresh vision and equipped for new heights in prayer. Through their influence thirty-seven other leaders attended the conference, all from Chinese-Asian churches in nearby cities.

What Pastor Alan and his church could not achieve in their private prayer times, they have now experienced beyond their imagination, together on their knees. Great joy fills this congregation as they now have learned to bring their gloves and bats and to play a winning "ball game" in united prayer.

Endnotes

1. Randy Frazee, *The Connecting Church* (Grand Rapids, MI: Zondervan, 2001), p. 43.
2. Frazee, p. 85.
3. Wayne A. Meeks, *The First Urban Christians: The Social World of the Apostle Paul* (New Haven, CN: Yale Univ. Press, 1984), p. 78.
4. From a speech given by Lyle Schaller at a Leadership Network Conference in Ontario, CA, October 1998.
5. Gene Getz, *Praying for One Another* (Wheaton, IL: Victor Books, 1983), p. 11.
6. Michael Griffiths, *God's Forgetful Pilgrims* (London: InterVarsity Press, 1978), p. 23.
7. Griffiths, p. 24.

Chapter Eleven

Renovate Your Prayer Closet

few months ago my wife and I were touring Scotland, enjoying the many castles and palaces of my historic motherland. While visiting the Palace of Holyroodhouse in Edinburgh we noticed a portion of the historic royal residence identified as the "Queen's Closet" and the "King's Closet." We anticipated a lavish collection of royal robes, fancy shoes, and other exquisite clothing accessories. What we discovered proved to be a point of intriguing biblical significance, especially as it relates to the role of prayer in the local church.

When this palace was built, a "closet" was not a little storage area for the safekeeping of clothes, as we understand it today. Rather, it was a special meeting room. To be called to the "King's Closet" in that day was a rare privilege, indicating you were part of an inner circle of close acquaintances or special guests.

One reason well-meaning Christians in the local church stay away from prayer meetings is their conclusion that the biblical ideal is to focus on the private "prayer closet" Jesus spoke of in Matthew 6:5-13. Many have assumed that our Lord had in mind a small cubicle for individual prayer. The fact is that when the 1611 King James Bible used this term it likely indicated the kind of room we discovered at The Palace of Holyroodhouse. For most of us today, it may be time to reconstruct and expand our prayer closet. The result will be a balanced and flourishing prayer life.

Jesus Evaluates Prayer Groups

Jesus provided various metaphors and examples to teach us the importance of corporate prayer. The following passage from Matthew 6 often is misunderstood. People even use this passage as proof text for praying alone rather than in community. Like all Scripture, we need to study the passage.

> "And when you pray, do not be like the hypocrites, for they love to pray standing in the synagogues and on the street corners to be seen by men. I tell you the truth, they have received their reward in full. But when you pray, go into your room, close the door and pray to your Father, who is unseen. Then your Father, who sees what is done in secret, will reward you. And when you pray, do not keep on babbling like pagans, for they think that they will be heard because of their many words. Do not be like them, for your Father knows what you need before you ask him.
>
> "This, then is how you should pray:
>
> "'Our Father in heaven,
> hallowed be your name,
> your kingdom come,
> your will be done
> on earth as it is in heaven.
> Give us today our daily bread.
> Forgive our debts,
> as we have forgiven our debtors.
> And lead us not into temptation,
> but deliver us from the evil one.'" (Mt. 6:5-13)

Notice the context. Here Jesus compared three groups in prayer.

Group A—the Pharisees. Jesus called them hypocrites. They prayed with the wrong motive. Prayer was their opportunity to appear religious and to be thought of as spiritual. Jesus stressed the priority of a God-centered, rather than man-centered, motive.

Group B—the Pagans or Gentiles. Jesus exposed the pagans' fervent but repetitious and trite prayer pattern. They prayed with a misguided method. He cautioned His disciples not to follow their pattern.

Group C—the Disciples. As Jesus instructed His followers He envisioned the days when their gatherings to pray would be part of their lifestyle. He wanted them to pray with pure motives and effective methods.

> *The pronouns are all plural in the pattern of prayer Jesus taught.*

Jesus began this landmark prayer lesson with an obvious supposition and an important insight when He states, "and when you pray." He assumed their prayer gatherings would be a regular part of their spiritual development. The pronoun here is plural, so He is talking about a group—the disciple group. In our language it would be "when you guys pray" or "when y'all pray" (in southern dialect). In other words, Jesus says, "When you all pray together as my followers, do it this way in your gatherings—not like those praise-hungry Pharisees or misguided Gentiles."

To prove the point, the pronouns are all plural in the pattern of prayer Jesus taught. He did not give the instruction to pray: "*My* Father who art in Heaven . . . give *me* this day *my* daily bread, and forgive *me my* sins, lead *me* not into temptation, but deliver *me* from evil . . ."

This was a teaching passage on the motives, venue, and pattern of corporate praying in the lives of Jesus' followers. This was a prayer pattern designed primarily for gathered believers, not an isolated disciple in a "prayer closet." Yes, there are also some singular pronouns in the passage, which demonstrate that even corporate prayer is still a very personal experience of communion with God.

Expanding the Closet

When Jesus said, "go into your closet to pray" (KJV), just what did He mean? This word, *tameion*, appears in the Greek New Testament four times. Among those instances it can mean "inner rooms" (Lk. 12:3, NASB) or a "storeroom" (Lk. 12:24, KJV, NASB, NIV). The New International Version, New American Standard, and New King James all use a clearer idea when they describe this place of group prayer in Matthew 6:6, calling it a *room* or *inner room*. One thing is clear: The narrow interpretation of a private chamber for solitary prayer is not a necessary or reasonable meaning. This would be especially difficult when Jesus speaks to a group of disciples, using plural pronouns. It would either be a very crowded private closet with many sweaty and cramping disciples—or it must mean a place large enough for a corporate gathering.

The obvious historical application of this principle is seen in Acts 1:12-2:1 where the disciples are gathered in an upper room, out of the public eye, enjoying extended group prayer. This pattern continued in Acts as they responded to persecution (Acts 4:23-31), engaged in intercession for an imprisoned leader (12:12-17), and sought the Lord's direction for ministry (13:1-3). This was their regular experience in the closet.

Prayer Out of Balance

Over the centuries the American church has wandered far away from the priority of community experiences of prayer. We have tended to do so under the banner of the private "prayer closet" even though Christians in many Eastern cultures cannot understand why American Christians insist on praying alone.

Over the years church members have asked, "Which is more important—private prayer or corporate prayer?" I tell them, "Yes!" Both are essential. It is like asking which leg is more important for walking. Right and left are absolutely necessary.

In my own journey I have found that private prayer has brought depth and insight to my corporate prayer experience. Corporate prayer has brought breadth and motivation to my private time with the Lord. Frankly, I cannot imagine living a vibrant and balanced

Christian life without a regular weekly dose of both. Those who neglect the consistent habit of praying in extended fashion with a community of believers are robbing themselves of great blessing and balance. In a sense, they are trying to hop on one leg and finding the prayer journey difficult, at best.

> *In the recent centuries the church has wandered far away from the priority of community experiences of prayer. We have tended to do so under the banner of the private "prayer closet."*

Learning Like the Early Christians

I am a member of a network of churches that emphasizes "the prevailing church." Based on Acts 2:42, the network encourages every congregation within the association to pursue impact through a balanced ministry of teaching, fellowship, breaking of bread, and prayer. Of the four, the last is least emphasized. A church cannot truly "prevail" in an authentic New Testament sense unless there is a clear definition and implementation of the prayer component in the life of the church.

The lack of clarity and implementation in prayer was illustrated when I attended a conference at one of the flagship "prevailing churches." I asked the leadership of the church about how prayer was being practiced corporately, how individuals were learning to pray and how a life of prayer was affecting every dimension of ministry. The pastoral staff noted a successful effort in which hundreds of people were signed up to pray in hour-long solitary assignments all round the clock, seven days a week.

This sounded exciting. So in good faith, I made an appointment with the volunteer prayer coordinators of the church. They gave me a different story. The fact was most of the 168 time slots were not filled. Many who signed up were not fulfilling their duties. The volunteer prayer leaders were very discouraged. They longed for the pastoral staff of the church to set the pace through their example and felt quite disheartened by the overall lack of emphasis on prayer by the leadership.

I concluded that until we are clear and serious about the prayers of Acts 2:42, the best we could boast of is "almost Acts 2:42" churches.

Many believers struggle in learning how to pray. Hundreds of volumes have been written over the centuries on the theology and practice of prayer. Yet, the most fundamental principle has often been neglected: Young Christians must learn to pray in community with mature believers. Prayer is a vital part of discipleship and corporate prayer is indispensable as a part of the process.

> *Young Christians must learn to pray in community with mature believers.*

In Acts 2:42 we see the discipleship patterns that emerged immediately in the Jerusalem church, comprised almost entirely of new believers. It says, "They devoted themselves to the apostles' teaching and to the fellowship, to the breaking of bread and to prayer." You could not learn the apostles' doctrine by subscribing to "The Peter, James, and John Tape-of-the-Month Club." You had to be gathered in community. The same was obviously true of fellowship and the breaking of bread. And how did they learn to pray? Together.

In the Greek, Acts 2:42 literally reads, "the prayers." The definite article is a strong argument for prayer as a vital stand-alone activity, not a tack-on for the other three corporate disciplines. These prayers were not just a blessing added to the beginning and end of Bible study. These early Christians gathered exclusively for prayer. In all likelihood they followed the pattern Jesus set forth, which led them through themes of worship, submission, intercession, supplication, warfare, and praise. In extended seasons of corporate prayer they learned to pray effectively.

Joining the "Community" in the New Testament Closet

A few years ago an elder in my church expressed his refusal to attend prayer meetings with two objections. "First," he stated, "we are not to pray to be seen by men. Secondly," he declared, "we are to go into our prayer closet." His conclusion was that the Bible clearly taught that it is better to pray alone than with other Christians.

My response was twofold. First, I asked him to change his motive and come to the prayer meeting. I encouraged him to seek God, not impress people. Secondly, I explained that it was time for him to renovate his prayer closet, because it was much too small according to biblical standards.

Private prayer is a wonderful discipline. When coupled with regular, extended times of dynamic corporate prayer it can lead to a beautiful, balanced spiritual journey. For those who struggle, it is time to run on both legs toward the prize of prayerful, abundant living for Christ. There is a community of gathered Christians—on their knees and ready to help.

CHAPTER TWELVE

Explore the Possibilities

*P*raying churches are diverse and beautiful, like snowflakes, fingerprints, and personalities. My model has been to grow prayer through exciting, passionate, worship-based prayer. As churches have sought God in this way, people have had fresh encounters with the living Christ! As a result, their lives have been changed—and the church has changed as all these people who have encountered Jesus Christ, either for the first time or in a fresh way, begin sharing that with their friends and neighbors.

Out of this model, as people have encountered Christ through prayer, they want to develop in other aspects of prayer as well. As they see exciting prayer modeled in a prayer meeting with others, they take what they have learned into their personal prayer lives as well. They also become prayer entrepreneurs. Over my years at Arcade Church, we saw the number of prayer ministries and opportunities grow to dozens. Why? Because people revived by prayer have gotten a burden to start a prayer ministry that ministers in a particular area. That will likely happen in your church as well—though it takes a long time to develop.

The danger in reading books like this—that seem to be based on "what worked in my church"—is that you might attempt to implement a prayer strategy that looks like another church's.

Prayer ministry is best accomplished by inspiration, not imitation. The Lord will direct you into strategies that work for you and your setting. I firmly believe in the scriptural importance of corporate prayer and would challenge any church to do what it takes—even if it is a huge struggle—to develop a powerful corporate prayer meeting. But this chapter is designed to stimulate your creative juices in considering the possibilities of other prayer ministries. Some churches grow prayer and a hunger for God one prayer opportunity at a time. You can use these ideas either as supplements to your corporate prayer meeting, or as starting points to a broader prayer ministry. But I warn you: Deep down people want to connect with God. If some prayer ministries do not give them that opportunity, your ministries will not grow—and will eventually fade out. Seek God for where to begin. The Lord will make your prayer expression a unique tribute to His glory.

Prayer ministry is best accomplished by inspiration, not imitation.

Form vs. Reality

In prayer and in life it is important that we learn the difference between "form" and "reality." Form involves the shape and details of the methods we use. Reality speaks to inform us what is actually happening—in our setting the reality is whether or not people are praying.

One of my favorite stories from *Reader's Digest* tells about a man who ordered an expensive suit for a banquet. As he left the tailor's shop, a sudden rainstorm doused the jacket and shrank one of the sleeves. "We can't do anything about it today," the tailor told him when he returned to the shop. "Just stretch the sleeve over your hand, and no one will notice."

With his arm contorted the customer left the shop and once again was doused by rain. This time, a pant leg shrank. "I can't take care of that now!" exclaimed the tailor. "Pull the bottom of the pants over your heel, and nobody will notice."

His body twisted, he again left the shop. Two women were passing by. "That poor man!" said one. "I wonder what's wrong with him?" "I don't know," said the other. "But he sure is wearing a nice suit!"[1]

This man's "reality" was the desire to look good for the banquet. Unfortunately he became so consumed with the "form" of that particular suit that he missed his objective. In prayer ministry it is easy to try to acquire the effective methods and appearance used by a church for prayer. However, we need to find the suit that fits us in our situation based on the kind of church, leadership team, and opportunities available to us.

Some prayer strategies function well at one location but not at another. Every place is different. At one church where I served we hosted frequent all-night prayer meetings. In recent years, I have not conducted any all-night prayer times but have adopted other exciting approaches to prayer. There are many forms to facilitate the reality of prayer.

You need to find out what works for your situation. Developing creative activities and expressions for prayer is a process of experimentation and scheduling. Be free to learn and explore as the Lord leads. Two excellent resources that I recommend to help you strategize are: *My House Shall Be a House of Prayer*, Jonathan Graf and Lani Hinkle, editors (NavPress 2001) and *The Prayer Saturated Church*, by Cheryl Sacks (NavPress 2004). Here are some possibilities to consider.

There are many forms to facilitate the reality of prayer.

Powerhouse Prayer Meetings

I remember reading the story of two young men who arrived early to a service at the Metropolitan Tabernacle in London to hear Charles Spurgeon speak. As they waited to enter the auditorium, a man approached and asked if they would like to see the power-generation room of the church. Not wanting to be rude, they complied. The gentleman took them to a downstairs door and opened it to reveal a packed house of people gathered for prayer prior to the service. "That, my friends, is the power source of our church." With that he extended his hand and introduced himself. His name was Charles Spurgeon.

What is a "powerhouse" prayer meeting? It is a specific prayer time that occurs prior to or during a worship service (or other event where the preaching of God's Word is taking place).

This can be a good place to start a prayer ministry because it occurs at the same time people attend church. Prayer for the pastor and the Sunday services should be the strategic focus for this prayer time. For it to be effective, you need to continually keep guard so the focus doesn't change. Because of their experience with group prayer, most people, through a lack of understanding, will take prayer meetings right to people's needs. You're praying fervently for the empowering of the Holy Spirit for your pastor. It is getting intense and passionate. Then all of a sudden, brother Bill begins to pray for his sick sister. The Spirit-inspired passion is broken! You will need to continually educate the people who come to pray as to the focus for which they are to pray. Make sure, though, that there are opportunities to pray for people's needs elsewhere. Those with brother Bill's heart, too, need a place to pray for that.

Early Watch

The early watch format is intended for those who can meet early in the day. For years I attended a men's prayer meeting at 6 a.m. on Monday mornings. Arcade Church's women's morning prayer group meets Saturdays at 8:00 a.m. Another early watch might focus on the needs and specific prayer requests of missionaries around the world. Two others pray for leadership and church staff. Again, notice that each is focused on a specific theme or topic. Why? If you look at the times of corporate prayer in Scripture, all are narrowly focused (see Ezra 8:21-23; 2 Chronicles 6-7; and Acts 12:5 as examples). We can better pray in agreement (the powerful biblical concept put forth in Matthew 18:19-20) when we are not jumping all over the place with everyone's agenda.

Affinity Group Gatherings

Prayer meetings that have a common interest and stage in life are one way to form age-group gatherings. One of the best known is Moms In Touch. Mothers have formed various prayer groups oriented around their common stage in child rearing. Singles, teenagers, and various church departments can easily form weekly prayer groups at church.

I've seen a seniors' prayer group that meets on Wednesday nights during the traditional prayer meeting time they were used to attending for many years. These seniors cherish this regular occasion to worship and pray.

Concerts of Prayer

Concerts of prayer are periodic events involving the whole church in a unique setting and style of praying. They are usually facilitated from the platform and involve a variety of expressions through small group prayer, large group prayer, and personal intercession. I have led them on Sunday mornings, Sunday evenings, and midweek. We often conduct concerts of prayer for our church and for a gathering of churches from around the community.

Appendices A-H offer a variety of guides for leading a concert of prayer.

All-Night Prayer Meetings

An all-night prayer meeting can extend from 6, 9, or 10 p.m. to 6 a.m. In a sense it is an extended concert of prayer. But it functions best when a wide array of expressions including lively worship, prayerwalking, interactive small group prayer, scheduled breaks and (very) energizing refreshments are planned. If you are starting out with these nights of prayer, while you should encourage people to try to attend the entire thing, make sure they know that they are welcome even if they can only attend a portion of it. The worker who gets off from second shift at 11 can come then; the person who goes in to work at 7 Saturday morning, and needs to sleep to do her job, can leave at 10 p.m., and so on.

Prayer Chains

Prayer chains are another form of praying together. I saw twenty-four-hour continuous prayer chains where one person calls another to pray, that one calls the next person, and then the next person calls and so on. Each person contacted prays for an hour. It is like a tag-team on the phone. There is a mutual sense in which people pray together.

The more standard prayer chain is an intercessory-oriented focus where special needs are transmitted from one person to the other by phone. Prayer chains are not a good foundation for a prayer ministry because they do not provide the opportunity for people to pray together, encourage one another, or learn to pray effectively in community. Everyone is left to pray solo. They are also a challenge to maintain and administer. But, they can be a good supplement to a broader prayer movement. They can also be an easy outlet for needs praying.

All-Church Weekly Prayer Meetings

Many churches have done this, historically, on a Wednesday night. Brooklyn Tabernacle is famous for its Tuesday night prayer meeting. I found it beneficial to take some of our leaders to New York to experience the Tabernacle's format and to stimulate their vision. Each week I lead an all-church prayer time, similar to Jim Cymbala's.

This is a worship-based prayer time with extended, free-flowing worship in the early segments. Often the gathering will include a devotional. We may pray for prayer requests submitted by the body (submitted ahead of time, not during the meeting) and for particular church decisions. Sometimes we pray for a person's healing, hear testimonies, or pray for visiting pastors or missionaries. No two times are alike. This involves great sensitivity to the Holy Spirit's leading and praying as He directs. A sample format is featured in appendix H.

Many people call the prayer meeting an oasis in the middle of the week. They would not miss it—their favorite service, a prayer meeting. Imagine that! We have experienced many blessings, personally as a church, which we believe are directly attributed to the Fresh Encounter. This is a form that may work for you.

If you want to see this model in action contact either Grace Church in Eden Prairie, Minnesota (where I pastor now), Arcade Church in Sacramento, California, or Strategic Renewal International (www. strategicrenewal.com) for information on how to attend a worship-based prayer meeting or a three-day Prayer Summit.

Home Prayer Cells

Prayer does not have to happen in the church building. It can also occur in homes. These should be worship-based payer meetings led by trained and experienced facilitators.

One model is called "Lighthouses of Prayer." People gather in their homes to pray for their neighbors. Then they ask their neighbors if they have any requests explaining that a group prays for their neighborhood. It is surprising how open nonChristians are to prayer.

Twenty-four-hour Prayer Center/Call-in Line

For many years my former church in Sacramento has sponsored a World Prayer Center. We reserved a room in the church just to intercede for others, our church, community, and the world. In that room there is no shortage of material. There are books on prayer, videos on prayer, and a cassette player with dozens of praise music tapes. There are books listing our entire church membership in alphabetical order; as well as books with all the children and youth in the church listed. Also, there are books listing churches in town, books focused on praying for the least-evangelized mega-cities of the world and books describing how to pray for Muslim countries. There are maps of the United States, the world, the unreached peoples, the 10/40 Window and more on the wall. Participants can visually locate the area for which they are praying. Other prayer notebooks include elders and their prayer requests, staff prayer requests, and current prayer needs of the church membership.

One walks into the prayer room and begins with worship. It might be one person and an accountability partner or a friend or a family praying together. The prayer room is a great place to take children and teach them about worship-based prayer; play a praise tape, sing, and learn to enjoy the Lord together as a family. Take your pick from all the ways you can pray together. You can pray about anything in the world.

We have a phone call-in line that is not your typical "dial a prayer." It is a dedicated line. You call in and leave your prayer request. If someone is there, they take the request and write it down. Sometimes they answer the phone and pray with the caller. If no one is present, there is an answering machine 24 hours a day, taking requests. The next person in the prayer room records the request and prays. All requests are kept for two weeks and prayed over by each person who visits the prayer room within those two weeks. It is wonderful to know that there are people dedicated to praying over a request every day, every hour for two weeks.

The point to a twenty-four-hour prayer room is to provide a specific opportunity and priority of prayer and to elevate prayer to the place of honor it deserves. Also it gives people an additional opportunity to pray together. This format requires a lot of organizational oversight but can be a great blessing to the church.

Prayer Partners

This is a one-on-one ministry of people who become prayer partners. The partners meet regularly and pray. The partners can be someone we meet at our lunch break, someone from the neighborhood with whom we exercise, or a friend from church. The idea is to form friendship and accountability by praying together on a weekly basis.

Prayer Visitation Teams

This ministry is vital as these teams visit people who need prayer. It encourages the hospitalized, shut-ins, or others who need an extraordinary touch of prayer. This team visits people and prays for those who would like to attend church but cannot.

This form could bless many in our fellowships. We, especially our older saints, live in a lonely culture. What a wonderful time all could experience praying and enjoying rich fellowship at the throne of grace. That may be our ministry of united prayer.

Prayer Retreats

This familiar format involves days away reserved for prayer with applied teaching in a retreat format. This combination of instruction, inspiration, and implementation is a good place to whet the appetite for prayer.

Prayer Summits

Summits consist of a group of people getting away to a retreat center for multiple days to pray. There is no agenda and no teacher except the open Scripture and the Holy Spirit. They were started by Dr. Joe Aldrich and Multnomah Bible College. Aldrich wanted to take pastors from a given community to a retreat center to pray together. They felt this would bring unity to the pastors and their churches within a community. If it worked well for pastors, why not for a church body? In the last decade we began to implement this approach in the local church setting with powerful results. This is another practical way to apply corporate prayer in various forms but requires skilled facilitation by mature, trained leaders. There are certain guidelines we have discovered as crucial for the effective flow of the Prayer Summit format.

Prayerwalking

Prayerwalking has been described as praying "on-site with insight." You can prayerwalk around your neighborhood, workplace, church campus or any area. Some congregations send their people overseas to prayerwalk in an area difficult to reach with the gospel (this is called a prayer journey).

> *Prayerwalking has been described*
> *as praying "on-site with insight."*

My first prayerwalking experience came during college as a friend and I walked through a graveyard. Of course, we were not praying for the people buried there, but I will never forget how moving it was to think of life's brevity and God's eternal reality.

I know an attorney who facilitates weekly prayerwalking on the grounds of the state capital. Once a quarter, our church walks the campuses of several public schools on a Sunday evening, praying for the staff and students. The possibilities are endless as people take a walk with Jesus, worshiping, and calling on His name for needs that become apparent.

Prayer Driving

This is a form of the same idea, except it is done with groups in vehicles and typically covers a broader geography. I know an elder in our church who organizes people to drive through various neighborhoods to pray. Sometimes they organize "drive by praying" to span the periphery of the entire metropolitan area.

Leadership Prayer Support

Leadership prayer support is a specific ministry of prayer for the church leadership and their families. One of the common formats is Pastor's Prayer Partners.

This initiative usually involves men who pray for their pastor every day. There are many variations of method. Typically, these men will meet with the pastor throughout the year for training, motivation and intercession. This can involve a regular breakfast gathering or an annual retreat, as I do with my men.

We also have a women's ministry known as S.W.A.T. (Spiritual Warfare Attack Team). These women pray aggressively for leadership and their families. This prayer support is dedicated to praying for my wife, my children, and me. They know that if the devil cannot destroy the pastor, he will go after his wife and family. Their calling comes into play at this very point.

Prayer Chat Rooms

Using today's technology, some are beginning to use a "chat room" on their website for a corporate prayer time. This works well when there is a clearly identified facilitator. Even this can be a worship-based time, initially focused on praise and thanksgiving. We want to be sure that we have some ground rules about who participates and how it will function.

Great Possibilities and Core Principles

Of course, we are just scratching the surface with these suggestions. The Lord will guide you into various versions of these ideas or provide other forms to use.

I want to underscore the importance of trained leaders to facilitate these prayer experiences. You will also want to consider how every prayer expression can be a worship-based experience. More training materials are available through www.StrategicRenewal.com.

The rest of the book is dedicated to the specifics of refining your facilitation skills and learning the dynamics of worship-based prayer. Get ready to lead your people in a fresh encounter with Christ!

Endnote
1. *Readers Digest*, (January 1995), p. 68.

PART FIVE

Keeping the Encounter Fresh

CHAPTER THIRTEEN

Prayer Gatherings That Keep Going, Going, Going . . .

Nothing kills a heart for praying together in a church quicker than dead, disjointed, depressing prayer meetings. Earlier I referred to those classic weeknight prayer meetings I grew up attending. A few dead songs preceded a disconnected devotion. Then came the dreaded question: "Does anyone have any prayer requests?" This was followed by at least thirty minutes of the most depressing updates including Aunt Matilda's ingrown toenails, Uncle Charlie's slipped disc, Cousin Bill's car problems, Sister Bertha's heartaches over her unemployed husband, and all the latest chitchat about the church. More often than not this observation followed: "Oh, we're out of time again, we'd better hurry and pray."

As a rule what ensued was pretty banal most of the time. I like to call it the "bless . . . be with" syndrome. It went like this, "Bless this, bless that, be with him, and be with her . . . in Jesus' name, amen." And with that, the "prayer meeting" was over. It certainly was. If that was the essence of communion with God, it was over all right. I stopped attending, like ninety-five percent of the rest of the congregation.

A different paradigm—the worship-based, seeking God prayer meeting—on prayer meetings is needed. In this chapter, I will explain how to develop and lead these exciting, dynamic prayer gatherings. Later we will explore the dangers that can put prayer meetings "in the tank."

Regardless of the prayer meeting type you lead, certain dynamics are essential to the effective function and longevity of these gatherings. Here are some keys that will help you guide a dynamic prayer time:

An Equipped Facilitator

In most ministries of the church, we like to be sure the leaders are capable, gifted, and trained to do an effective job. Bible teachers receive training and need a solid working knowledge of the Scriptures. Children's workers generally have regular orientation and are guided by policies that keep the ministry to kids excellent and safe. Choir members are expected to have basic music talent.

> *Nothing kills a prayer ministry quicker*
> *than dead, disjointed, depressing prayer meetings.*

For some reason when we need a leader for a prayer meeting, the attitude can be, any warm body will do: "Let Charlie do it. He's got nothing else to do. He's a really nice guy, and boy is he faithful." What a great approach for killing the prayer ministry!

That is why I dedicate so much of my time as a pastor to training committed, competent, and confident prayer leaders. With the right training, biblical understanding and sensitivity to the Spirit of God, these people will ignite prayer ministries throughout the church and community. The prayer leaders I've trained have led thousands of others in dynamic experiences of seeking God's face and watching His hand do the unbelievable.

An Effective Method

Fortunately, Jesus did not leave us adrift on a sea of human opinion as it relates to a pattern for effective prayer gatherings. Amid life's rush and among the rut of "how we always did things," we forget His basic pattern. Like Marge, a lady in my church said, "A good thing about memory loss is that when I see reruns on television, they're all new to me."

We do not need to experience memory loss in our prayer meetings. I want to introduce you to a new way of looking at our Lord's pattern for prayer meetings.

The "4/4-Time" Pattern of Prayer

This simple, balanced approach has given many a prayer leader the handles they look for to follow a biblical pattern of prayer.

In recent years I've shared this pattern with thousands of prayer warriors in seminars and various other settings throughout my travels. Without fail, it provided a new enthusiasm for prayer and became a pattern that works for people who struggled previously.

The diagram below is patterned after the 4/4 musical beat. It is the motion a director often uses in leading a musical performance. As a prayer tool it is an effective way by which the Holy Spirit can direct our hearts in a balanced and biblical format of communion with the Lord.

The Upward Stroke—Reverence

In the prayer pattern Jesus gave His disciples, He urges us to begin with a focus of worship. ("Our Father in heaven, hallowed be your name. . . .") We call this upward focus the "Reverence" stroke.

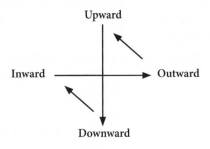

In the normal course of prayer ministry, effective prayer is worship-based, not need-based. It begins with the character of God as we take time to focus our entire beings on the wonders of who God is. He is the "Father" with whom we have a secure and loving relationship through Christ. Yet, He is "in heaven" as the sovereign and great God, ruling the world by His might and wisdom. His name (and character) is holy and set apart from everything else in this world.

To enjoy this segment, do not ask God for anything. Instead, *give* to Him the glory and honor due His name in a spirit of biblical and heart-felt worship. To accomplish this, read the Psalms or other portions of Scripture. Revelation 1, 4, and 5, Daniel 9, Nehemiah 9, and 1 Chronicles 29 contain some great thoughts for worship.

Focus on the attributes of God mentioned in these passages. Some commonly available tools used to guide our focus are the listings of the names of God, attributes of God, and names of Jesus. Encourage participants to lead out in songs of worship. Praise Him from the heart for who He is, giving His name reverence. If available, have a worship team lead—though find a way to still allow for some impromptu singing and Scripture reading.

The Downward Stroke—Response

Jesus taught a second element of biblical prayer when He said, "your kingdom come, your will be done on earth as it is in heaven. . . ." This stroke is our response to God's character in prayer. During this segment we yield to the control of the Holy Spirit and we recommit to God's kingdom purposes. Introspection and surrender mark this time of response. Pledge obedience to the will and Word of God, desiring that His perfect will be accomplished in our lives. Confession could be a part of this segment.

The most practical tool for this stroke is an open Bible. The will of God is the Word of God. The best way to talk to God about His purposes is in His own words. Having just reverenced the Lord in worship, respond to His character and plan through His Word. The psalmist prayed: "Direct me in the path of your commands, for there I find delight. . . . Your word is a lamp to my feet and a light for my path" (Ps. 119:35,105).

> *The will of God is the Word of God. The best way to talk to God about His purposes is in His own words.*

In yielding to the Holy Spirit, we read God's holy Word in the holy communion of prayer that we might fulfill His holy will.

Here someone will often read a passage of Scripture—or pray it—as God lays it on his or her heart. Many times, after a scripture is read, others spontaneously pray parts of the passage or verse back to God.

The Inward Stoke—Requests

"Give us today our daily bread. Forgive us our debts, as we also forgive our debtors." This is the next element Christ teaches in His model prayer. This involves a period of heartfelt requests with the themes of provision and purity.

Of course, Jesus had just said our Father knows our needs before we ask (Mt. 6:8). This is not a time of informing God of our needs as much as it is a conscious trust in God as the perfect definer and provider of our needs. During this stroke, pray about personal requests and the concerns of others. I would also encourage and teach people to pray kingdom prayers for those outside the church—the lost. Do not take requests here. Rather, look for ways to get people to simply pray. Put them in small groups, hand out slips of paper with a request (taken ahead of the meeting) on each one. Also, remember matters that are more corporate in nature, such as congregational challenges or broader issues in the body of Christ. In all this recognize that, "My God will meet all your needs according to his glorious riches in Christ Jesus" (Phil. 4:19).

In this section the prayer leader often directs from the platform: "Let's get into groups of four, men with men and women with women, and pray about . . ."

A prayer journal or request list is useful during this stroke to keep track of needs and a record of God's answers. It is important to remember the Request segment follows Reverence and Response. As Jesus said, "If you remain in me and my words remain in you, ask whatever you wish, and it will be given you" (Jn. 15:7). Only after we have truly worshiped and surrendered our wills to God do we have the proper perspective on our needs.

Not only is God's provision a key concern during this stroke, but so is purity. We commit ourselves to lives of purity and forgiveness, living with a clear conscience before God and man. We pledge to seek and extend forgiveness daily. Purity is the key to harmony and unity in the body of Christ and must not be neglected in our prayer times with the Lord.

The Outward Stroke—Readiness

While we would love to stay in the posture and pleasure of prayer all day long, we must get off our knees and into the daily battle. The outward stroke reminds us of the spiritual contest before us and, more importantly, reassures us of the spiritual resources within us.

When we pray, "Lead us not into temptation, but deliver us from the evil one," we recognize our own inability to overcome the temptations and attacks of daily life. We entrust our welfare in the warfare to the delivering power of our Divine Enabler.

This can be a time of meditation and memorization of God's Word as we gird ourselves with the sword of the Spirit and prepare to counteract personal temptation and spiritual attack. This is exactly what the Savior did. By having the "treasure of truth" stored in our hearts and ready on our lips, we trust in His victory to carry us through the day.

The Upward Stroke—Reverence

This model of prayer concludes on the same note it began—on a high note of praise. Like the modern version of the Lord's Prayer that we recite, "for Yours is the Kingdom and the Power and the Glory forever. Amen."

After giving our attention to reverential worship, submissive response, thoughtful requests, and spiritual readiness, it is natural to finish with a strong reminder of our awesome God to whom

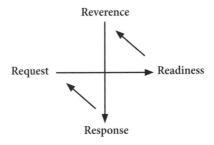

we pray and in whom we trust. His kingdom is unshakable; His power, unmatched; and His glory, unimaginable. Through time spent with Him, we experienced a foretaste of His majesty.

Closing this final stroke with songs of praise and declarations of His promises brings us full circle.

With effective leadership in a biblical and balanced approach, we avoid mindless and meaningless prayer times. Try to follow the "4/4 time" pattern of prayer, not rigidly, but as an overall pattern for a variety of prayerful expressions. As the Holy Spirit takes the role of "conductor," let Him turn your struggle into a symphony of balanced, biblical prayer for your soul's good and God's glory.

For more information on the 4/4 pattern to pray from Scriptures, see my book *PRAYzing!* In it is 26 captivating stories on what this kind of prayer looks like in a local church setting.

One Life Is Changed

Many times when churches try to move from needs-focused to God-focused corporate prayer meetings they come under criticism. People get concerned that if they neglect to pray for people's needs, they won't see answers to prayer, they won't see people's lives changed. But that is an absolutely false assumption. We see many examples in Scripture where an intercessor in the midst of a problem approaches God but never mentions the problem (see Nehemiah). And amazingly the problem gets taken care of.

Jeremiah 29:11-13 tells us that all we have to do is seek God together (Jeremiah 29 is a corporate passage) and He will show us His plans for us. Jesus tells us not to worry about everyday things.

Just seek the kingdom of God, and all these things will be taken care of (Mt. 6:25-33). It will happen in your church as well—even if everyday needs praying is given less emphasis. Seek God together, and everything else will get taken care of!

Mary Ann's Discovery

Worship-based prayer comforted and strengthened Mary Ann Carlson in a troublesome time. Something she unconsciously searched for eluded her even after she became a Christian. When people invited her to prayer meetings, she always went. One time people gathered together, but prayed privately. She bowed on her knees in a crowded living room. She attended prayer retreats, but returned home plagued by constant emptiness.

Mary Ann did not know what to expect at her first Prayer Summit. Later with profound joy she realized, "This is what I have searched for for so long!"

Worship-based prayer prepared her for mounting pressures when she faced her husband Jerry's diagnosis with dementia. She endured fear, anger, denial, and the questioning why stages. The Lord took her through each step and opened the way for her to know Him deeply.

Whenever she could, she participated in corporate prayer. Tired and thirsty, she found solace in praise music and prayer, allowing them to wash over her. This gave her strength to care for Jerry.

Soon after a Prayer Summit, Mary began attending a women's prayer meeting at church on Saturday mornings. Her husband died about eight years later on a Friday. The next day she went to the meeting and shared her sorrow. Finally, at the last Prayer Summit she released all the memories and hard times she faced during her trials.

Worship-based prayer caused Mary Ann to focus on God and His sovereignty in making life changes. She applied what she learned in private and corporate prayer. Without the church's prayer ministry of biblical, balanced communion with the Lord, she still would be searching.

CHAPTER FOURTEEN

Hindrances to Avoid

*J*onathan Graf tells the story of a time when he watched a prayer leader valiantly try to direct a prayer meeting into seeking God, only to see it taken from him time and time again.

The ministry this leader worked for was having a day of prayer. In the afternoon session, the leader, Steve, tried to teach the forty or so people gathered there in the Prayer Summit model of prayer. He gave explicit instructions on how they were to operate. This was going to be a time of praise, focusing on the attributes of God. They could read a Scripture, start a song, pray a prayer of praise.

They began. Within two minutes someone started praying for their neighbor's child. Steve tried to bring it back with a gentle reminder of the theme. Within a minute someone else was off on some prayer need on their heart. Then another and another. Steve stopped the group and went through the instructions again. Then they started once more. But soon the meeting was again away from its focus and onto needs. He tried once more to rein it in, but to no avail.

As we have mentioned before, even with good leadership it can be difficult keeping the prayer meeting focused—and Steve was a good leader. Therefore, as you venture into this new paradigm, you need to be very aware of the hindrances to good prayer meetings—and do your best to avoid them.

Poor Instructions

To avoid the many hindrances to an effective prayer meeting, good, clear instruction must be given as you share in the experience. Good instruction keeps prayer meetings from falling into a rut.

I've always enjoyed these examples of unclear instructions:

- On a Sears' hair dryer there was a label that read, "Do not use while sleeping."
- On a bag of Fritos it says, "You could be a winner. No purchase necessary. Details inside."
- A hotel shower cap box says, "Fits on head."
- On the bottom of a tiramisu dessert box was printed an especially "effective" label, "Do not turn upside down." Too late!
- On the packaging for a Rowenta iron it says, "Do not iron clothes on body."
- On a Korean kitchen knife, it says, "Warning, keep out of children."
- On an American Airlines pack of peanuts, the instructions read, "Open package, and eat the peanuts."
- On a child's superman costume, "Wearing this garment does not enable you to fly."

These warnings demonstrate that some people do not grasp clear instructions. These dear folks sometimes attend prayer meetings. I know, I've prayed with them.

In corporate prayer our instructions need to be especially clear. The better we understand what the Lord wants in an effective prayer time, the more it impacts the ministry of the church and helps our leadership.

Lack of Foundation

I was leading a seminar on this material one day in San Jose, California, when a lady interrupted, "Whenever I go to a prayer meeting at our church, I always try to pray first. Otherwise, all those long-winded people take over. If you don't speak your mind right way, you'll never get a word in edgewise."

There are more people than you would imagine with a similar attitude toward prayer. You need to set the foundation clearly. Just like any solid structure, prayer meetings need to have a good foundation or they won't go anywhere.

So where do we start? Participants need to be taught to pray from the Scripture, talking to God in His own words. We begin every prayer meeting with an open Bible. Most often, we begin by turning immediately to a Psalm. After reading through the passage, I ask, "What does this Psalm tell us about God—His character, His attributes, His ways?"

Participants need to be taught to pray from the Scripture, talking to God in His own words.

For the next few minutes we discuss Him, not our problems, opinions, or agendas. This sets the foundation for the prayer meeting. Once I have a sense that we have introduced a solid focus, we begin to pray. We do not ask, but give. We give Him praise, worship, and thanksgiving. I usually say, "For the next ten minutes you cannot ask God for anything—only give Him what He deserves. If you ask for something, a trap door will open under your seat." Of course, this is a joke, but it underscores the seriousness of matter.

Participants offer praise to the Lord in short sentence prayers based on the Scriptures. Some will start out with a song related to the text. This fits the pattern of the upward stroke of "reverence" based on the revelation of His Word.

As Christians we can tend toward compartmentalization in our walk with God. We think of our Bible reading as something we do in one corner and our prayer time as an activity separately enjoyed in another corner or at another time. Never the two shall meet.

Where did we get that idea? Both exercises of prayer and Bible reading are essential to communing with God. It gets exciting when we blend both into one dynamic experience with God.

The right foundation for prayer is God's Word, because that is where the instructions are. John 15:7 says, "If you remain in me and my words remain in you, ask whatever you wish, and it will be given you." The biblical foundation for prayer is essential because the instructions are explicit. Before we ask of Him, we adore Him. Face first, then hand.

We need to set the pace as leaders by showing people how to do it. We want to blend the reminder of God's character from the Word with singing spiritual songs, choruses, and hymns. Our method sets the pace. Focus on God, His worthiness, faithfulness, love, and countless other attributes.

Lack of Fervor

Another hindrance we encounter is a tendency for the prayer meeting to become dull and predictable. It can even become difficult to stay awake.

I remember reading a list of excuses to give the boss when you happen to be sleeping at your desk:

- "They told me at the blood bank this might happen."
- "Whoo! Boy I guess I left the top off that white out. You probably got here just in time."
- "I wasn't sleeping. I was meditating on the mission statement and envisioning a new paradigm for our company."
- "Somebody must have put decaf in the wrong pot."

My favorite is to wake up and say, " . . . In Jesus' name, amen."

Isn't that the way some prayer meetings feel? Someone wakes up just in time to say, "In Jesus' name, amen."

What can be done to change the slow, lifeless prayer meeting? If we are going to lead a prayer awakening in our church we must remember that prayer is ineffective apart from the Holy Spirit.

Let's be honest. We do not naturally have fervor, passion and zeal. In our flesh, we are incapable of bringing the necessary energy to prayer. But we do know the One who will generate that fervor we so desperately need. The Holy Spirit ministers to us in our weakness. He shows us how to pray.

> In the same way, the Spirit helps us in our weakness. We do not know what we ought to pray for, but the Spirit himself intercedes for us with groans that words cannot express. And he who searches our hearts knows the mind of the Spirit, because the Spirit intercedes for the saints in accordance with God's will. (Ro. 8:26-27)

What an incredible impetus to lead prayer under the direction and power of the Holy Spirit. He enables us to pray with passion and direction according to the will of God.

Elsewhere, Paul reminds us that it is the love of the Holy Spirit working in us to impart a passion in prayer (Ro. 15:30). The Spirit knows the deep things of God and communicates insight to us though spiritual thoughts and in spiritual words (1 Cor. 2:9-13). We are commanded to be under the Spirit's control, with the result being ardent, dynamic worship (Eph. 5:18-20). Sadly, we still try to pray without a conscious reliance on the Holy Spirit.

> *The Spirit of God is our personal indwelling prayer tutor.*

I like to remind prayer participants that the Spirit of God is our personal indwelling prayer tutor. It is vital during each prayer time, (usually in the "response" segment, after worship) to prayerfully yield to the Spirit of God. As you surrender your heart to His control you show others how to pray. The prayer meeting is purposeful and passionate.

I often provide leadership by praying something like:

> Lord we thank You for the Spirit of God. As we continue in our prayer time, we thank You that You know us—our needs, our thoughts, and our desires. Show us Your will and make Your word come alive. Apart from Your rule in our hearts, we are unable to pray effectively. We thank You

that You live within us and You are going to provide energy and insight as we pray.

Lack of Faith

Praying in faith cannot be emphasized enough. Without active faith we are "going through the motions." There is a sense of lifeless routine. Without faith, prayer becomes drudgery and a waste of time.

The writer of Hebrews tells us that "without faith it is impossible to please God, because anyone who comes to him must believe that he exists and that he rewards those who earnestly seek him" (11:6).

James reminds us that it is "the prayer offered *in faith*" (Jas. 5:15, emphasis added) that will bring restoration, healing, and forgiveness to our lives. Jesus stated that, "all things you ask in prayer, *believing*, you shall receive" (Mt. 21:22, NASB, emphasis added). Why even lead a prayer time if you are not going to pray in faith.

This underscores the importance of the foundation of worship from the Word of God, because faith comes from hearing and hearing by the Word of God (Ro. 10:17).

Remind participants regularly of the importance of praying in faith in response to the Word of God, trusting the God of the Word, through the aid of the Spirit. This is not just religious raucous, this is spiritual reality. I've often prayed in line with the father of the ill son, "I do believe, help my unbelief."

One other tool to cultivate faith in your prayer time is a focus on thanksgiving. So many times in the Bible we find God's people thanking Him for His mighty acts in the past as an incentive to trust Him for His provision and direction in the future. Psalm 52:9 says, "I will praise you forever for what you have done; in your name I will hope, for your name is good. I will praise you in the presence of your saints." Psalm 64:9-10 tells us that in considering "what He has done," the "righteous man will be glad in the LORD, and will take refuge in Him; and all the upright in heart will glory" (NASB).

For twenty years I've led a Sunday early-morning prayer time, typically beginning at 6 or 6:15. In recent years, a dear godly couple, Owen and Lois Baser, has participated. Lois has contributed great encouragement to the faith of our group. Every week she reflects on the issues we prayed over the week before. She recounts the answers God provided. Then, with a lively faith, she expresses trust in the Lord for the day before us. That's the way to pray. I hope you will lead your people accordingly, in great faith, as you come before the Lord.

> *"It is not the greatness of my faith that moves mountains, but my faith in the greatness of God."*

A plaque I owned several years ago offered some profound wisdom. "It is not the greatness of my faith that moves mountains, but my faith in the greatness of God." Prayer meetings established on the foundation of worship from God's Word move upward in faith. We are not mustering up an emotional optimism. We are magnifying the One who is the object and originator of our faith. That's the way to pray.

Chapter Fifteen

More Hindrances Than You Might Think

I t may seem strange that I would include such specific instruction about overcoming hindrances to effective prayer. You might be asking, "Can't we just all get together and pray? Why do we need to follow certain patterns and guidelines?" Those are fair questions.

First, it is a false assumption to think that we all know how to pray well. The disciples admitted their inability when they asked our Lord to teach them to pray (Lk. 11:1). Paul admitted his weakness in prayer in Romans 8:26. Since most Christians spend such small amounts of time in prayer, and most churches pray so little, we must not be particularly proficient.

When it comes to corporate prayer, the dynamics get even more unpredictable. Everyone in attendance is at a different level of maturity and understanding. Some pray well. Others, frankly, pray wrong and not according to the Bible. Some are extroverts and carelessly verbose while others are withdrawn and shy.

I've seen many come with a personal agenda that can be self-centered and distracting. Political activists sometimes attend and want to pray on various partisan issues. Others carry heavy burdens, deep bitterness, or even a bad attitude. We have had a mentally ill visitor who is off his medicine interrupt many a prayer meeting. Others have bad theology, and somehow find ways to pray it. You never know what might happen at a prayer meeting where these unpredictable variables are present.

After leading corporate prayer meetings for twenty years several times every week, I have seen it all. Sometimes, I failed to lead effectively. My many mistakes, various successes, and the truths of God's Word taught me much about prayer. Let me share more of what I discovered.

Interesting Characters

Light attracts bugs. Sometimes prayer meetings can attract a wide array of interesting people.

Someone sent me a list of how to drive people crazy:

- At lunchtime sit in your parked car and point a hair dryer at passing cars. See if they slow down.
- Page yourself over the intercom without disguising your voice.
- Find out where your boss shops. Buy exactly the same outfit. Wear it one day after your boss does. This is especially effective if your boss is the opposite gender.
- Put mosquito netting around your cubicle at the office.
- Every time someone asks you to do something, ask, "Do you want fries with that?"
- Encourage your colleagues to join in a little synchronized chair dancing.
- Put your garbage can on your desk and label it "IN."
- Reply to everything someone says with these words: "That's what you think."
- Ask people: "Are you male or female?"
- Finish all your sentences with "in accordance with prophecy."

After reading this list I think all of these people have been in prayer meetings I have led.

Lack of Focus

When a prayer meeting lacks focus, there are no clear themes. The experience becomes muddled. This lack of synergy drains on prayer's effectiveness—and begins to bore the participants.

I teach leaders that God hosts the prayer meeting, but trusts us to guide it. As in most other areas of ministry, He always uses Spirit-led leadership. We have the responsibility to keep prayer meetings focused. This is one of the bigger problems.

We can rest knowing that the biblical pattern of prayer encourages specific areas of focus (Ezra 8:21-23; 2 Chronicles 6-7; Acts 4:23-31; Acts 12:5). This is clear from what we studied and why we learned a biblical pattern of prayer. It encourages united themes for prayer. Be sure of this, if you do not direct the focus, the impulses of people will.

> *When a prayer meeting lacks focus, there are no clear themes. The experience becomes muddled.*

It may sound like a contradiction since we said earlier that the Spirit of God is sufficient for every believer. However, we need to remember also not everyone in that prayer meeting is always in tune with the Spirit of God. There are times when people's impulses take the prayer focus "into a ditch." As leaders, we need to watch for that, and guard the moving of the Spirit.

For years I prayed every week with a dear brother, a church officer, who had an incredible passion for Turkey (actually it was a different country). With a marvelous missionary heart every time he prayed he tried to take us to Turkey. During worship he praised God for His presence in Turkey. When we surrendered to the Spirit, he remembered how the Spirit had moved during his last visit to Turkey. When we confessed our sins, he confessed our lack of compassion for people in Turkey. When we prayed for our Sunday services, his heart was attending church—in Turkey. If I had not led those prayer times with a clear focus, we would go to Turkey every time. Do not get me wrong. I love the country of Turkey, but there are hundreds of other countries, and other things of importance as well that also need prayer.

He was one of many who attend prayer meetings with an extraordinary burden or unique passion. If I did not lead with a clear focus, the prayer time would become a tug-of-war over personal agendas.

Let me give you three practical thoughts about finding and establishing focal points in prayer.

Be Specific

Remember the 4/4 time illustration? With these areas of focus in mind, lead the way and make it clear where you want to go. Will you focus on worship, surrender or praying for the church leadership? All of these are good. Just make it clear. You do not want to be like the fellow who said, "There goes a fine group of people, and I must catch up to them for I am their leader." That is backwards. Leading in the Spirit does not mean going with the flow—often the flow is not Spirit-led.

One key principle I learned is that the larger and newer the group, the clearer we need to be. When I lead a smaller group of folks who pray together every week and are well-versed on the idea of biblical, balanced, worship-based prayer, I do not have to give a lot of instruction. When I am leading a group of people new to the concept, I am more specific and directive.

The larger and newer the group, the clearer we need to be.

When I lead a large group in prayer, like our Fresh Encounter, I direct it in a hands-on way. You never know who may wander into one of those meetings when there are hundreds of people. You do not want to subject the direction of several hundred people to the agenda of a tipsy visitor or partisan activist—or a brother with a deep love for Turkey.

Be Illustrative

Make sure the group understands where you are going. Do they have adequate time to enter into the focus? Give them handles for participation. This requires communication. Let me illustrate.

Let's say we are worshiping, and the theme of God's beauty surfaces. I decide to make that a point of participation. While remaining with my head bowed in an attitude of prayer I will say, "Let's focus on the beauty of God. In just a moment, I want you to tell the Lord, in one sentence, why He is beautiful to you. I want you to pray, 'Lord, You're beautiful to me because . . .' and finish the sentence. As you are thinking about this, let's sing that first verse of 'O Lord, You're Beautiful.'"

As we sing this chorus, people can think about a heartfelt and specific response. Then as the song subsides, I repeat the instruction so everyone clearly understands, then ask them to begin. Most people appreciate this kind of specific focus and communication. It gives everyone a point of entry including the shy ones and newer believers.

Be Sensitive

How do you move from one focus to the next? Keep your Bible open. Listen to the Scripture readings, songs, and prayers. Look for a theme. Try to stay ahead a few steps.

Sometimes a clear theme will not emerge. It is okay to select one. At this point some prayer leaders get anxious. They wonder, "Should we pray for the lost in our community or the missionaries abroad? Should we pray for the elderly or the children?" In most cases I say, "Yes." It is all good.

If the Holy Spirit has not impressed on you a clear focus, I do not think the Spirit will be quenched if we pray for the missionaries rather than the local community and the children instead of the elderly in this particular prayer time. I think He is delighted that we are praying. He enjoys it, and we are edified, when we pray in agreement. If the Spirit has a specific, significant prayer agenda for you, He will move you to that theme.

A side effect of this focus in corporate prayer times is that it provides an opportunity to teach people to focus in their private prayers as well as in groups. The leadership you provide will help them understand how various themes can work and how different prayer dynamics connect.

Lack of Flow

Sometimes we get everyone initially focused but cannot keep the group heading in a direction with a spirit of agreement. It is this sense of praying in concert that brings a flow to prayer time. People can build on one another's prayers.

Continuity is a word that captures the essence of flow during prayer. Continuity fosters participation. People are able to connect with each other in unity and agreement. Focus eliminates a scattered experience while flow cultivates agreement and edification.

> *Continuity fosters participation. People are able to connect with each other in unity and agreement.*

I usually encourage three guidelines for continuity. I call them the "ABCs" of continuity.

1. Audible. To experience agreement, we need to be able to hear one another. Those with a soft voice will need to work harder to speak up. I like to kneel in prayer meetings. But, if I am not careful, only the Lord and the seat cushion hear my prayers.

Now this can be a cultural issue. If you were in a Korean prayer meeting, you would hear them praying aloud at the same time. But in Anglo culture most of us are not as used to that. So we pray one at a time audibly.

2. Brief. Nothing tends to hinder the flow of a prayer time quicker than long, drawn-out, scattered prayers. There are times you want to ask, "Does your train of thought have a caboose?"

I enjoyed praying with a seasoned saint, who is one of my heroes. Well into his eighties, he still attends several prayer meetings a week. Unfortunately, he tends to pray very long prayers during which many people lose their concentration. Some doze off.

I learned to sit next to him. This helps increase his awareness. He knows that if he goes longer than is comfortable, I will place my hand on his shoulder. If he keeps going, I will pat him on the back. He gets the hint and gives others an opportunity to pray.

This must seem horribly rude or aggressive. However, the goal of the prayer meeting is God's glory and mutual edification. "Let all things be done for edification" (1 Cor. 14:26, NASB). Long-winded folks can really hinder this. Encourage prayers that are no more than one to two minutes in length.

3. Clear. Remind people to pray for one thing at a time, not the whole truckload at once. Encourage prayers that stay on the theme. Continuity works when we stay on target with specific, direct prayers.

The prayer time can flow with agreement as we complement each other's prayers. The key is to be audible, brief, and clear.

Listening is also important for continuity. As we listen to God's Word being read and referenced, we are prompted to pray in agreement. As we hear the Spirit speaking through the hearts of others in prayer, we can agree with them.

A final aspect of "flow" is timing. Proverbs 15:23 says, "A man has joy in an apt answer, and how delightful is a timely word" (NASB). This is true in seasons of prayer. Someone may have a sincere burden for an issue or a scriptural insight that would be appropriate for prayer. The key is to be sensitive as to *when* it is best to pray for that issue. Find a time when it flows well with the direction of the group.

Through experience, training, biblical insight and with the aid of the Holy Spirit, you can facilitate seasons of prayer that are inviting and inspiring. However, there are still more hindrances to overcome. We will look at those next.

CHAPTER SIXTEEN

Still More Hindrances

*U*nlike a Sunday morning service, where in most churches it is inappropriate to call out something uninvited, most people view prayer meetings as less formal. They get used to being able to say things—and in the worship-based Fresh Encounter, they are even encouraged to do so. But it is difficult for people to learn what is from the Spirit and what is their own flesh wanting to speak out. Many a prayer meeting has been damaged by someone blurting out the wrong thing at the wrong time. Even more have been damaged by people thinking they have a "word from God" to share, when He hasn't given one. Satan loves to derail prayer meetings.

Effective group prayer is not a matter of blurting out random ideas, spiritual or otherwise. As we saw, a prayer meeting to which people will keep coming has a solid foundation of biblical worship, is fueled by faith, and is given clear focus out of which comes a flow. Now we look at two final obstacles.

Lack of Freedom

God loves diversity. He never designed two of anything exactly alike. Every person, animal, fish, tree, plant, planet, and star is a one-of-a-kind. On the other hand, man is a manufacturer of mass-produced copies. That is why He is called the Creator and why we have to watch our tendency to push conformity and sameness.

I am a strong believer in diversity of expression in prayer within biblical confines and in the interest of edifying participants. Without this freedom, prayer times become rigid and stifled. If variety and diversity are not allowed in a prayer meeting, the group will never grow larger than just those who like the format that is used. If it doesn't grow, it will soon decrease in size and effectiveness.

Scripture offers many ways to pray. Interestingly, sitting in a pew or on a folding chair are absent from the scriptural record. The Bible shows people praying with hands uplifted, and then flat on their faces in the same service (Neh. 8:1-12). Biblical prayer can be offered silently (Hab. 2:20), with a broken heart (Ps. 51:17), or in shouts and songs of joy (Ps. 69:30, 107:22). We can pray standing (Ps. 33:8, 135:2), kneeling (Lk. 22:41), lifting our eyes to heaven (Jn. 17:1), or bowing our heads (2 Chron. 20:18). And this is hardly an exhaustive list of the various options. Prayer should not look like a bunch of religious statues coming off the manufacturing line.

I hate to be blunt, but no matter how conservative the church, in a prayer time we should never thwart *any* of these expressions—unless of course the leader has asked for everyone to be silent before the Lord and sister Sarah decides it's time to start shouting! These expressions are all biblical. Some of them—ones that many churches either outright do not allow or at least frown on—even appear to be biblical commands. If we do not allow for the expressions the Holy Spirit moves our people toward, then we will quench the Spirit of God in our gatherings. When that happens the passion wains, people get bored, and the meeting dies.

Encourage a vertical focus.
I remind our people to pray to an audience of One. I tell them, "You are offering a solo to God while the rest of us are your back-up choir. We're not to conform to a particular style or model. We pray to enjoy Him."

The first time I attended the Tuesday night prayer meeting at the Brooklyn Tabernacle, I was surprised by how dim the lighting was. As I entered into prayer, I realized that my focus was directed to my personal time with the Lord rather than observing other well-lit participants. Whether you prefer bright lighting or a subdued feeling, the focus should be the same. We need to direct people to the vertical focus. It is imperative to take their eyes off the horizontal concern of what others may or may not be doing.

I remind our people to pray to an audience of One.

Give latitude for different worship expressions.
I learned that it is important to give participants liberty to enjoy appropriate, biblical freedom in prayer. I remind them, "You can stand. You can kneel. You can pray with your eyes closed or open. Feel free to stand, walk, sit, kneel, or bow low to the ground."

My children tend to express their love to me in a variety of ways. My oldest boy expresses himself best in writing. I probably have twice as many letters from him as from the other two put together.

My second son expresses his love physically. When he was young, I would sit quietly, working or watching television. Before I knew it he would be on my lap, messing with my hair. Even to this day, in his early twenties he thinks nothing of walking through the store with his arm around me.

My daughter is more verbal. She will say, "I love you, Dad" more readily than the other two.

The glory of my fatherhood is the diversity
with which my children express their love.

I do not tell my older son to hug me more. I do not insist that my second son become more verbal. I do not ask my daughter to write more letters. No. The glory of my fatherhood is the diversity with which my children express their love. Let this be a picture of the joy our Lord receives when his children are free to express their love, worship, and prayer in a meaningful and free fashion.

We want unity and flow, but we do not want people to feel restricted. Of course, their expression must be genuine but sensitive. It is never good to disrupt the flow or distract everyone else by some insensitive eruption of personal emotion. We should never allow anything that takes the attention off of God and puts it on an individual. But in most cases, if they want to kneel, stand, raise their hands, sit on their hands, cover their eyes, open their eyes, whatever, it is all right. That is part of the form that is beautiful.

Lack of Faithfulness

A final, serious hindrance to an awakening of effective prayer is a lack of faithfulness. We know how easy it is to be inconsistent and unreliable.

One such employee declared his dedication in these words, "I always give 100 percent at work—twelve percent on Monday, twenty-three percent on Tuesday, forty percent on Wednesday, twenty percent on Thursday and five percent on Friday."

I have learned that nothing damages the momentum of a prayer group more than the leader's inconsistency. Faithfulness to the prayer meeting needs to be modeled by the leader.

Over the years I noticed an interesting dynamic. If I am the leader of a regular prayer time and happen to miss a week, the next week we have a much higher absentee ratio. That is the way people are. It is probably better not to start a prayer meeting than to initiate it and flake. Jesus told us to count the cost before we start to build (Lk. 14:28-30). Finish what you start.

When I know I will have to miss a prayer gathering, I communicate the details to those who attend so they know I did not sleep in or forget. My faithfulness communicates the priority and passion of prayer to my fellow believers.

Conversely, nothing discourages the heart of a leader more than the unfaithfulness of the participants. Encourage consistency among your group not for human reasons alone, but ultimately because He is worthy to be sought. If we operate under the Spirit's discipline, and through the power of grace it will be a joy for the leader *and* participants.

> **Don't expect a big crowd when God is the only attraction.**

While lack of faithfulness can be discouraging, it is good to remember the reality of A. W. Tozer's words (paraphrasing): "Don't expect a big crowd when God is the only attraction."

Briefly, I would challenge you to the following points to avoid the hindrance of unfaithfulness.

1. Be consistent and enduring. Remember your vision "to die on your knees." As prayer leaders, we need to trust God for the grace to be reliable and consistent every week, year after year, decade after decade. Prayer is not a casual experiment. Prayer ministry is not a sprint but a marathon.

2. Be enthusiastic and positive. There is nothing worse than a leader who acts as if he has been sucking on pickles. I've attended prayer meetings where the leader said something like this, "Well, glad you're here this morning. I'm sure tired today. How about you? Whew, I could hardly get out of bed. Well, let's hope for the best and try to pray, if we can stay awake." Now that is uplifting!

We are there to meet with the Lord. We enjoy the privilege to seek His face, experience His presence and enjoy His marvelous provision. That's worth being excited about.

> *The only enduring motive for prayer*
> *is that He is worthy to be sought.*

3. Encourage the priority of the pure motive. I cannot say it enough. Remind participants they are not there to get an award pin for faithful attendance. We are not trying to earn God's approval. We are enjoying the means of grace He has provided in order to know Him more intimately. The only enduring motive for prayer is that He is worthy to be sought. He will be worthy next week, next month, next year, next decade, and for eternity. What better reason to keep showing up!

After the 9/11 crisis church attendance and participation in prayer meetings swelled. We tend to pray more in crisis. Our gracious God answers crisis-born prayers. When Peter cried, "Help Lord!" as he sank in the waves the Lord did not say, "Sorry Peter, you forgot the 4/4 pattern of prayer!" He rescued Peter. As a matter of pattern, however, it is imminently better to pray out of conviction. That is where the real blessing comes.

What are the convictions of a praying leader, a praying believer, and a praying church? In summary:

- God is worthy, far beyond the attraction of anything this world offers.
- I am needy, in spite of my apparent self-sufficiency and earthly prosperity.
- Jesus Christ invites me to seek Him and will empower me by His grace to endure in my pursuit.
- Jesus longs for His church to be a house of prayer, and I will faithfully contribute to that vision.
- Jesus' glory in and through the church to the world will be my determined passion.
- God is a rewarder of those who seek Him diligently.

With conviction, we cry, "Lord, teach us to pray!"

The Fire of a Fresh Encounter

*T*hree businessmen attended a work associate's funeral. They found it intriguing that the many friends and family who passed the casket gave a brief personal comment about the significance of the man's life. At the reception following they asked each other, "What would you want people to say about you when they walk by your casket someday?" The first of the three replied, "I would like them to comment on my commitment as a hard-working employee." The second noted, "I would like people to remember me as a good husband and father." After deep thought the third, said, "I would like them to look down at me, point their finger, and say, 'He's still breathing!'"

Alive and Awake

When future generations look back at this era of the history of the church, I pray they will know that we were still breathing. But I do not simply want the church to be alive. Even a patient on life support is "alive."

I pray we will be fully awake—thriving, not just surviving. I pray we will be experiencing life-changing fresh encounters with the living Christ—enjoying and exhibiting His glory.

Even though much of the research indicates that the American church is drowsy, I am not content to keep hitting the snooze alarm.

In Revelation 3:1-3, Christ pleads with the church in Sardis. He appeals for an honest status check. He calls them to repentance from drowsiness and a return to fresh spiritual desire.

> I know your deeds; you have a reputation of being alive,
> but you are dead. Wake up! Strengthen what remains and
> is about to die, for I have not found your deeds complete
> in the sight of my God. Remember, therefore, what you
> have received and heard; obey it, and repent. But if you do
> not wake up, I will come like a thief, and you will not know
> at what time I will come to you.

Throughout the book, we've been speaking of fresh encounters with Christ in the context of united prayer. We've taught about life-changing moments in His presence. All this leads to a genuine awakening. In the past, our nation has experienced some great awakenings of spiritual vitality through extraordinary movements of prayer and Spirit-empowered preaching of the Scriptures. No doubt, we need a similar awakening today. I believe the Lord is calling us to "wake up."

"Wake up! Strengthen what remains, and is about to die."

Join me in praying, "Lord, let the awakening begin today in me and in my church." It starts with an obedient, God-seeking leader who embraces a vision for corporate prayer, is motivated by God's worthiness and desires to experience Christ's glory with His supernatural community, the church.

The awakening builds through a deepening understanding of the "community culture" of the early church's model as presented by Jesus' teachings and the New Testament prayer commands.

The awakening blossoms as more called and trained leaders

provide expanding opportunities for a broad experience of biblical, balanced prayer while modeling a lifelong passion for God's glory in the church.

Could It Be?

By nature, I am an optimist. The elders of my church once told me, "Daniel, if you found a big pile of manure in the driveway, you would shovel through it exclaiming, 'There has to be a pony in here somewhere!'"

It is true. I always tend to find opportunity in opposition, possibilities in problems, and challenge in crisis.

In spite of my optimism, and spiritual gift of faith, I must admit that I am concerned about what I see in our society. On the surface America is the most prosperous and technologically advanced society in the history of the world. All seems bright. But the Bible reminds us that we are not to look on the things that are seen, but things unseen. Man looks on the outward appearance, but God looks at the heart.

In a spiritual sense, I see America as a vast, dark landscape upon which there is a lot of frenetic, generally fruitless activity. Things are growing darker and colder by the day. There are glimmers of light here and there. But on further investigation many are man-made flashlights, running on short-lived human batteries.

In search of hope, believers gather around in "flashlight fellowships." The various flashlights are new, clever, and quite interesting to many newcomers. But in the long haul the light and heat provided in this context is not sufficient.

Every once in awhile, you find a fire. It's the real deal. It was not created by human ingenuity or programming. It seems more a divine visitation; heaven-sent fire instead of human-made flashlights. People are warmed, enlightened, and changed forever.

Around the "fire fellowships" people lose their intrigue with the flicker of flashlights. They are looking heavenward in deep gratitude for the fire from above. They are hungry for more. They are concerned for the darkness in the land.

They invite wandering and weary friends in from the cold. Eventually, leaders from other parts of the dark prairie come to investigate those simple fires. By faith they put a stick in the fire through a fresh commitment to pray.

These meager fire-sticks are not as interesting as the flashlights, and are seldom reported in the papers and magazines. But in time these resolute people of prayer are able to get a fiery fresh encounter with Christ going back at their own fellowship. Things begin to change.

As they experience the fire, in large and small settings, a dream is birthed in the hearts of those who are discontent with the fancy flashlights. They long for a landscape ablaze with the fire. A warming fire. A fire of illumination. A healing fire. A transforming fire. A supernatural fire.

Could it be that the dark landscape of American society might soon be alight with heaven-sent fire? Can we envision a nation ablaze with a revival so glorious, so powerful that everything changes for good?

Hopefully this will be the day when no one cares about the personalities or programs involved in the spread of the fire. All hunger for human recognition gets consumed in the blaze. All glory is given to Christ.

We don't need more and better flashlights. We need a firestorm.

This is my ultimate vision. We do not need more and better flashlights. We need a firestorm. Could it be?

In answering that question my heart is encouraged by what the Lord told us about His heart and vision for this kind of awakening: "If my people, who are called by my name, will humble themselves and pray and seek my face and turn from their wicked ways, then will I hear from heaven and will forgive their sin and will heal their land" (2 Chron. 7:14).

"Is it not written, 'MY HOUSE WILL BE CALLED A HOUSE OF PRAYER FOR ALL NATIONS'?" (Mk. 11:17, emphasis added).

Amen. So be it! He is able!

Implementing Your Vision

*A*s I have traveled the country to speak in churches and at conferences, many Christian leaders ask, "What specific things should I begin to do to implement a fresh vision for worship-based prayer in my church?" This question has become so common I wanted to address it in these final pages.

Of course, there is no one perfect strategy. I only can offer suggestions that have worked well for me as I implemented this kind of plan as a senior pastor. If you work in a different ministry capacity, you may have to augment your approach.

Cast Vision and Equip Leaders

Many pastors have a tendency to preach on prayer and start a variety of new prayer initiatives right away. Yet, without a team of capable leaders around you with a strong foundation and a clear vision, many plans eventually will fizzle.

I have found that the best initial efforts should focus on finding those people whose hearts are prepared and who are ready to help lead a prayer movement. Invest in these people. The materials in this book came from that very commitment. I realized early in my ministry that I needed missionaries of change who understood the goals and were equipped to help. As I took time to clarify everything I had learned about implementing worship-based prayer in the local church, the ideas that comprise this book eventually emerged.

I suggest that you find a group of leaders (between 10 and 20 people) who are moved to pray. You can use whatever books or materials best capture and articulate what you want to occur to equip these leaders. If you use *Fresh Encounters* as a resource, you have several options:

- Have your team read this book. Then download the application questions available at www.navpress.com, and discuss them.
- Purchase the audio or DVD version of the "Fresh Encounters" seminar along with the workbooks that are designed for group study. These resources are available at www.strategicrenewal.com.
- Schedule a "Fresh Encounters" seminar at your church. We have an entire team of trained leaders available to speak at your church, most of whom are pastors who are skilled communicators and have implemented worship-based prayer in their churches. Contact us at www.strategicrenewal.com to schedule your seminar.

Make Sundays Strategic

I have found the first and best prayer time to initiate is an early-morning gathering on Sundays. For more than 20 years, I have met with a group of leaders and intercessors for 45–60 minutes of worship and intercession before church. We typically start 2½ hours before the first service to allow participants time to go back home to get ready or pick up their families.

The format is simple. We read through a psalm, take time to worship from the passage for about 15 minutes, then take a few moments to surrender our hearts and agendas to the Lord (following the 4/4 pattern described in this book). We then free everyone to prayerwalk the building. Intercessors will pray for the services, the various ministries of the day, and the people who will be coming. During the last 15 minutes, we gather again in the front of the auditorium where I kneel or sit (typically accompanied by the worship leaders), and the group gathers around to pray for us and for the services.

This prayer time has several strategic benefits:

- Knowing it is the Lord's day, pray-ers already are thinking about church and their involvement. Sunday is the most strategic day of the week with the broadest impact and must be bathed in prayer.
- It is a powerful time of prayer for the senior pastor as he is often in the final moments of his sermon preparation. My best applications often have come to me during these compelling prayer times.
- Few people have schedule conflicts this early in the morning.
- It prepares the way for prayer teams to meet later in the morning during the worship services for intercession. At my church, most leaders of these service intercession gatherings were trained at this early hour meeting. I also suggest that prayer times later in the day follow the same psalm and pattern, even including the prayerwalking.

Preach Toward a Catalytic Event

Certain big events are significant momentum builders for your church's prayer vision. Prepare a leadership team to help you organize and lead such an event, which could include:

- **Prayer Summits.** These watermark experiences do more to teach people how to pray than anything I've ever experienced. You will need to train facilitators in advance, find a functional retreat or conference center, have an administrative team, and promote the event aggressively.

Your church will never be the same after holding a Prayer Summit, and many people will begin to plug into weekly prayer times as a result of the transformation they experience.

- **Prayer Conferences.** Bring in experienced, passionate, gifted leaders who can encourage and equip your people in many aspects of their walk with Christ. Themes can include spiritual disciplines, learning to pray, women in prayer, men in prayer, praying for children, teaching youth to pray, etc. When I hosted prayer conferences like these at different churches over the years, it motivated and trained our own people. Even though many attendees came from other churches and states, the ultimate benefit was strong within our own congregation. In my new book with Dr. Elmer Towns, *The Church That Prays Together: Inside the Prayer Life of 10 Dynamic Churches*, we describe other churches that have hosted such conferences.

- **Prayer Field Trips.** Consider taking a group of intercessors on a field trip to other praying churches. I have taken many groups to The Brooklyn Tabernacle in New York over the years. As I already noted, "The heart cannot taste what the eyes have not seen." Whether it is Brooklyn or another dynamic praying church, this kind of firsthand exposure will ignite fresh vision and involvement in your church. Strategic Renewal is sponsoring this kind of experience several times a year from different places in the country. For information about an upcoming trip, please visit www.strategicrenewal.com. While you may not be able to be implement strategies on this scale, try to find a way to expose your people to a greater vision for what prayer can become in your own church.

- **Special Seasons of Intercession.** Many churches sponsor a week of 24/7 prayer prior to Easter or Christmas. Some participate in the Global Day of Prayer for 10 days leading up to Pentecost Sunday (see www.GDOPUSA.org). This approach helps people get a taste for prayer and can produce great blessings all around.

I suggest you conduct an instructional and motivational preaching series leading up to whatever event you hold.

Empower the Saints to Lead

You have countless options for the next steps to take in implementing your vision, many of which I describe in chapter 12. You'll find even more ideas in *The Church That Prays Together: Inside the Prayer Life of 10 Dynamic Churches*. The key is to keep training the saints, giving them powerful experiences and letting them initiate and lead the specific components of the vision. Encourage your motivated leaders to read Cheryl Sack's *The Prayer-Saturated Church*. This resource will help them understand the very practical realities of organizing and leading specific prayer ministries.

Recruit a Prayer Administrator

Even the best vision can be derailed and sputter into oblivion without a solid administrative structure. As a senior pastor, I always led the prayer vision, but I never organized or managed it. God was faithful to provide one or more individuals with administrative gifts who could handle organization, communication, coordination, and planning. I met with my prayer administrator regularly. It was one of the best investments I ever made for the sake of one of the most important ministries I ever led.

Ultimately the Lord will show you what to do next. I hope you will review the principles of this book often to keep your prayer vision fuelled. Most of all, I hope you will persevere with a passion to die on your knees. Christ's calling is clear. You are ever needy. He is always worthy to be sought.

If we do not cross paths on earth, I will plan to see you around God's throne as we bow together with all the saints and angels for the ultimate worship-based prayer time. Perhaps after a few million years of worship, we can stop and share stories of everything the Lord did in and through us as we sought His face on this earth and led His people into His glorious presence in His "house of prayer"—the church of the living God.

Seven Stage Concert of Prayer

*T*his format weaves worship and prayer through seven stages. Each stage of prayer maintains a particular focus. Below are suggested Scripture and song promptings that will enhance the prayer times.

Stage One: Reverence
A season of worship, adoration, and praise.

Scripture Promptings
1 Chronicles 29:10-12; Psalm 34:1-3; Psalm 95:1-7; Psalm 100; Psalm 104; John 4:20-24; Hebrews 13:15; Revelation 4:9-11; Revelation 5:8-14

Suggested Song Promptings
"Lord I Lift Your Name on High"
"Come Thou Fount of Every Blessing"
"I Worship You Almighty God"

Stage Two: Reflection

A season of soul searching and waiting on God in quiet communion with Him through His Word.

Scripture Promptings

Psalm 46:10; Psalm 62:1-2, 5-8; Psalm 131; Psalm 130:5-6; Psalm 139:1-18,23-24; Hebrews 4:12-13

Suggested Song Promptings

"Take Time To Be Holy"
"Open Our Eyes, Lord"
"Breathe"

Stage Three: Repentance

A season of acknowledgment and confession of sin.

Scripture Promptings

Nehemiah 1:4-6; Psalm 19:13-14; Psalm 51:1-5; Psalm 66:18; Proverbs 28:13; Isaiah 6:5; Isaiah 55:7; 2 Corinthians 7:11; 1 John 1:7-9

Suggested Song Promptings

"Search Me, Oh God"
"In My Life, Be Glorified"
"Give Us Clean Hands"

Stage Four: Restoration

A season of gratefully acknowledging the restoration of divine fellowship and pursuing the restoration of interpersonal fellowship.

Scripture Promptings

2 Chronicles 7:14; Psalm 16:11; Psalm 30:5; Psalm 32; Psalm 51:7-19; Mark 11:25; Ephesians 1:7; Ephesians 4:26-27,29-32; Colossians 3:13

Song Promptings

"More Love to Thee"
"My Jesus, I Love Thee"
"We Are an Offering"

Stage Five: Requests

A season of personal petition as well as intercession on behalf of other individuals and the church.

Scripture Promptings
Matthew 7:7; John 15:7,16; Romans 8:26-27; Ephesians 3:14-21; Philippians 4:6-7; 1 John 5:14-15

Song Promptings
"Sweet Hour of Prayer"
"What a Friend We Have in Jesus"
"Seek Ye First"

Stage Six: Renewal

A season of renewing personal commitments to spiritual growth, renewing the mind through the memorization of the Word, and renewing one's strength for the spiritual battle.

Scripture Promptings
Psalm 51:10; Isaiah 40:31; Romans 12:1-2; 2 Corinthians 4:16; Ephesians 4:23-24; Ephesians 6:10-18; Colossians 3:10

Song Promptings
"Take My Life and Let It Be"
"Have Thine Own Way"
"Lord I Give You My Heart"

Stage Seven: Rejoicing

A season of expressing our gratitude to God for His many blessings and undeserved goodness.

Scripture Promptings
1 Chronicles 16:7-36; Psalm 107:22; Psalm 118; 1 Corinthians 15:57; Colossians 1:12; Colossians 3:15; 1 Thessalonians 5:13

Song Promptings
"Great Is Thy Faithfulness"
"God Is Good All the Time"
"Give Thanks"

A.C.T.S. Model Concert of Prayer

Opening Songs and Opening Remarks
Brief inspirational comment on prayer
"Lord, Reign in Me"
Explanation of Concert of Prayer concept

Phase One—Adoration
Brief inspirational and explanatory thoughts on adoration

Adoration song package
"God of Wonders"
"We Will Glorify"

Adoration prayer focus
Prayer leader cues participants with various attributes of God
and an accompanying verse for each. Praying can be done in
small groups or individually.
All Powerful (Jer. 32:17, 27)
Omnipresent (Ps. 139:7-12)
Unchanging (Num. 23:19)

Holy (Rev. 4:8)
Loving (1 Jn. 4:8,16)
Merciful (Lam. 3:22-23)
Truthful (Ps. 117:2)
Longsuffering (Ex. 34:6-7)
Transition: "Holy, Holy, Holy"

Phase Two—Confession

Brief inspirational and explanatory thoughts on confession

Confession song package
"Cleanse Me Oh God"

Confession Prayer Focus
Participants are encouraged to spread throughout the auditorium for an individual time of personal confession, corporate confession, and national confession.
Transition: "One Pure and Holy Passion"

Phase Three—Thanksgiving

Brief inspirational and explanatory thoughts on thanksgiving

Thanksgiving song package
"Count Your Blessings"
"God Is So Good"

Thanksgiving prayer focus
Participants are encouraged to offer "popcorn" thanksgiving prayers to God via various microphones placed strategically throughout the auditorium.

Phase Four—Supplication

Brief inspirational and explanatory thoughts on supplication

Supplication song package
"Seek Ye First"
"I Need Thee Every Hour"

Supplication prayer focus
Personal Needs
Church Needs
Transition: "He Knows My Name"

Community/National Needs
Global Needs

Closing Comments and Song
"Bless The Lord, O My Soul"
"Shout to the Lord"

Four-Focus Concert of Prayer

1. A Focus on God—Praise

1 Chronicles 29:10-19; Psalm 18:1-3,30-36; Psalm 21:13;
Psalm 66:1-7; Psalm 86:8-13; Psalm 89:11-18; Psalm 99:1-5;
Psalm 136:1-3; Psalm 139:1-18; Psalm 145:1-21; Isaiah 55:8-9;
Romans 11:33-36; Jude 24; Revelation 15:3-4

2. A Focus on Ourselves—Purpose

Confessing our distraction
Mark 4:18-19; Luke 6:46; Luke 10:38-42; Hebrews 12:1-2;
1 John 2:15-17; Revelation 2:1-7; Revelation 3:14-22

Confirming our direction
Matthew 28:18-20; Acts 1:8; Mark 16:15; 2 Timothy 2:1-5;
2 Timothy 4:1-5

3. A Focus on Our Church—Passion and Vision

A hunger for God—that we might understand His passion and vision

Philippians 3:7-14; Isaiah 6:1-8

A burden for others—that we might have our heart broken by the same things that break God's heart
Matthew 9:35-38; Luke 19:41-44

4. A Focus on Our World—Peace

Praying for internal peace amid world turmoil
John 14:27; John 16:33; Jeremiah 33:6; Psalm 29:11;
Psalm 119:165; Isaiah 26:12; Philippians 4:7; Galatians 5:22

Praying for interpersonal peace as a beginning place
Romans 12:9-18; Romans 14:19; Ephesians 4:30-32;
1 Thessalonians 5:13; Hebrews 12:14

Praying for world leaders that we might live in peace
1 Timothy 2:1-8; Luke 2:14; Psalm 122

A Concert of Prayer and Communion

Welcome and Prayer

Season One: Who He is in view of the cross
A time of kneeling at the cross and giving heartfelt worship to Christ because of Who He is.

Worship in response:
Reading: "Glory in the Cross"
"When I Survey the Wondrous Cross"
"Here I Am to Worship"

Worship in the Word:
The Lamb: Isaiah 53:7; John 1-2:9; 1 Peter 1:18-19; Revelation 5:6-14; Revelation 7:9-17; Revelation 12:10-11; Revelation 14:1-4; Revelation 15:3-4; Revelation 17:14; Revelation 21:22-23
The Redeemer: Romans 3:24-25; 1 Corinthians 1:30-31; Colossians 1:13-14; Titus 2:11-14; Hebrews 9:11-14
The Savior: Luke 2:11-14; Luke 19:10; Acts 5:30-32; 1 Timothy 1:15-17; 2 Timothy 1:9-10; Hebrews 7:25

Worship in song:
"There Is a Redeemer"
"Hallelujah, What a Savior"
"Here I Am to Worship"

Season Two: Who we are in view of the cross

A time of kneeling at the cross and offering humble gratitude for our new life in Him.

Worship in the Word:
2 Corinthians 5:17-21; Romans 8:1,14,15,17; Ephesians 1:3-4,13; Ephesians 2:10,19; 1 Peter 2:5,9-11

Worship in response:
Reading: "God's Amazing Grace"

Worship in song:
"Amazing Grace"
"And Can It Be"
"We Are an Offering"

Season Three: How I live in view of the cross

A time of kneeling at the cross in quiet examination and genuine surrender.

Worship in the Word:
Romans 6:1-13; Romans 12:1-2; Galatians 2:20; Ephesians 5:25-27; Philippians 3:7-11; Colossians 3:1-11; 1 Peter 2:24

Worship in song:
"Create in Me a Clean Heart"
"Take My Heart (Holiness)"
"Have Thine Own Way Lord"

Communion:

Worship in song:
"Near the Cross"
"Lamb of God"

Worship in partaking:
"Forever Grateful"

Before the Throne of Grace Prayer Guide

"Let us therefore draw near with confidence to the throne of grace, that we may receive mercy and may find grace to help in time of need" (Hebrews 4:16, NASB).

Preparation for Prayer

Five important ingredients to effective, concerted prayer:

1. Use the **SCRIPTURE**—Learn to talk to God based upon His Word (Psalm 119:24,105).
2. Rely on the **SPIRIT**—Submit to the leadership and guidance of the Holy Spirit as you pray (Romans 8:26-27).
3. Be **SPECIFIC**—Keep your prayers targeted *to the focus of* particular themes for maximum agreement and continuity.
4. Keep your prayers **SHORT**—You will have many opportunities to verbalize your prayers so be careful not to pray too long at a time.
5. Be **SENSITIVE** as you pray—Listen to the Lord as He directs you in prayer. Listen to others that you might agree and complement their prayers.

Section One:

Drawing Near to the Throne of Grace—A time of worship and thanksgiving
- Reverencing the One who sits on the throne
  (Psalm 84:11; Revelation 4:1-11; Revelation 5:6-14)
- Rejoicing in the grace that flows from the throne
  (Romans 5:15-20; Ephesians 1:3-8; Ephesians 2:4-9;
  Ephesians 3:7-8; 1 Corinthians 3:10; 1 Corinthians 15:10;
  2 Corinthians 8:9; 2 Corinthians 12:9; 1 Timothy 1:12-14)

Section Two:

Receiving Mercy in Our Time of Need—A time of confessing our weaknesses, failures and sins before a holy, merciful, and forgiving God.
- 2 Corinthians 6:1-2; 2 Corinthians 12:10; Galatians 2:20-21;
  Hebrews 12:14-15; James 4:6

Section Three:

Finding Grace in Our Time of Need—A time of petitioning God for His grace in various areas of our lives.
- Grace to maintain pure and godly lives
  (Titus 2.11-12; Romans 6:1-23)
- Grace to be of one heart and one soul
  (Acts 4:32-33; Psalm 133; Romans 15:5-6; 1 Corinthians
  1:10; 1 Corinthians 3:1-11; Ephesians 4:1-6; Philippians
  2:14-15; James 3:10; John 17:20-26)
- Grace to give bold and compassionate witness of Jesus Christ
  (Acts 1:8; Acts 4:20,31,33; Romans 9:1-3; Romans 10:1;
  1 Timothy 2:1-8)
- Grace to give our resources sacrificially and joyfully
  (Acts 4:32-37; 2 Corinthians 8:1-5,7-9; 2 Corinthians 9:6-8)
- Grace to faithfully and powerfully minister via our spiritual
  gifts (1 Corinthians 12:4-7; Romans 12:3-8; 1 Peter 4:10)

A Guide for Evangelistic Praying

1. Our Praise

Take time to worship God for His hand of lovingkindness, mercy and grace, which has caused Him to offer His glorious salvation to mankind.

Psalm 25:1-7; Psalm 31:19-22; Psalm 36:5-9; Psalm 96:5; Jeremiah 31:3; Romans 5:8; Ephesians 2:4-5; 1 John 1:14-16; Ephesians 2:8-9; Romans 5:15; Titus 2:11

2. Our Purpose

Take time to affirm in prayer God's evangelistic purposes and ask His Spirit to fill your heart with the same intentions.

Matthew 28:18-20; Acts 1:8; Mark 16:15; Luke 24:47

3. Our Passion

Pray for a deeper passion. Confess any apathy. Ask for a revival of evangelistic zeal in the church.

Matthew 9:35-38; 1 Timothy 2:1-8; Romans 9:1-3; Romans 10:1; 1 John 17:2-26

4. Our Proclamation

Ask for boldness in proclamation and pray for others who carry God's Word to the unsaved.

Ephesians 6:18-20; Colossians 1:28-29; Colossians 4:2-6;
2 Corinthians 4:1-6; 2 Corinthians 5:20; Romans 15:30-33

5. Our Petition

Pray for specific lost souls that they would be open to the gospel and attentive to the Spirit's call.

A Guide to Praying for our Church

Praying for Our Church

Season One: "Lord, Make Us a Worshiping Church"
A Church with a High and Lofty View of God
1 Chronicles 29:10-12; Revelation 4:9-11; Revelation 5:8-14;
Psalm 46:10; Psalm 145:1-7; Isaiah 6:1-5

A Christ-Centered Congregation
John 1:1-5,14; Ephesians 1:15-23; Ephesians 3:20-21;
Colossians 1:13-20; Colossians 2:6-10; Revelation 1:4-18

A Church with a Sacrificial, Worshiping Heart
Acts 2:42-47; Acts 4:32-37; Romans 12:1-2; Hebrews 13:15-16

A Singing, Celebrating, and Reverent People
John 4:23-24; Psalm 95:1-7; Psalm 100; Psalms 146-150

Season Two: "Lord, Make Us a United Church"
A Church with the Mind of Christ
1 Corinthians 2:16; Philippians 2:1-8

A Church with No Divisions
1 Corinthians 1:10; 1 Corinthians 3:1-11,21-23; Philippians 2:14-15

A Church Pursuing and Maintaining Unity
Romans 15:5-6; Ephesians 4:1-6; Psalm 133; James 3:10; John 17

Season Three: "Lord, Make Us an Evangelistic Church"
Matthew 9:35-38; Matthew 28:18-20; Acts 1:8; Acts 4:13,20,31; Romans 9:1-3; Romans 10:1; 1 Timothy 2:1-8

Season Four: "Lord, Make Us a Praying Church"
Acts 1:14; Acts 2:42; Acts 6:4; Ephesians 6:18; Colossians 4:2,12; 1 Peter 4:7

Fresh Encounter

(Following is a sample of the format used our the weekly prayer service.)

6:25—Quiet music plays in darkened auditorium as screen displays a nature scene and Scripture
Quiet on the Set—prayer request slips handed out at doors as people come in; all songs on PowerPoint unless indicated otherwise

Scripture for the screen: John 15:8—"My Father is glorified by this, that you bear much fruit, and so prove to be My disciples."

6:45—Announcement is made and leaders available to pray with people; during this time rotate slides between Scripture and this announcement: Several of our church leaders are standing nearby and available *right now* to pray with you about any burdens, personal needs or special prayer requests you may have. Please feel free to approach them and enjoy this wonderful opportunity to pray together in trusting the Lord. "Don't worry about anything; instead, pray about everything" (Philippians 4:6, TLB).

7:00—Opening PowerPoint presentation for reflection and heart preparation; listen to "Knees to the Earth" (New Passion CD)

Sing: "In My Life, Be Glorified"; "Be Glorified in Me" ("You Set My Feet to Dancing . . ."); "As The Deer"; "I Delight in the Lord"

Praises and Prayer Time:
Note answers to prayer as handed in by congregation; prayer slips (requests from congregation, typed and duplicated—2 or 3 requests per slip); everyone prays out loud at the same time for needs written on slips.
Sing: "He Knows My Name"

Prayer Time for Other Churches and Ministries:
Pastor Carl Engle—Foresthill Community Church

Devotional Reflection: Pastor Daniel
John 15:4-11: "Abide in Me, and I in you. As the branch cannot bear fruit of itself, unless it abides in the vine, so neither can you unless you abide in Me. I am the vine, you are the branches; he who abides in Me and I in him, he bears much fruit; for apart from Me you can do nothing. If anyone does not abide in Me, he is thrown away as a branch and dries up; and they gather them, and cast them into the fire, and they are burned. If you abide in Me, and My words abide in you, ask whatever you wish, and it will be done for you. By this is My Father glorified, that you bear much fruit, and so prove to be My disciples. Just as the Father has loved Me, I have also loved you; abide in My love. If you keep My commandments, you will abide in My love; just as I have kept My Father's commandments and abide in His love. These things I have spoken to you, that My joy may be in you, and that your joy may be made full" (NASB).

Prayer Time for the Ministry:
40 Day Discovery; Personal Renewal and Direction; Congregational Vision; Clarity for Leadership—Post 40-Days; Harvest Festival (Community-wide Halloween Outreach); Christmas Outreach; Christmas Experience Committee—Strength and wisdom; Fresh vision for those far from God
Sing: "The Church's One Foundation" (All verses)

Closing Announcements (lights down in front)
Sing the closing song: "You Alone"